KURT VONNEGUT'S AMERICA

For Tom —
The conversation
continues.
Life is recess/
recess is life.
all best wishes,
Jerome
8/24/09

KURT VONNEGUT'S

AMERICA

Jerome Klinkowitz

The University of South Carolina Press

© 2009 University of South Carolina

Published by the University of South Carolina Press
Columbia, South Carolina 29208

www.sc.edu/uscpress

Manufactured in the United States of America

18 17 16 15 14 13 12 11 10 09   10 9 8 7 6 5 4 3 2 1

Library of Congress Cataloging-in-Publication Data

Klinkowitz, Jerome.
   Kurt Vonnegut's America / Jerome Klinkowitz.
      p. cm.
   Includes bibliographical references and index.
   ISBN 978-1-57003-826-6 (cloth : alk. paper)
   1. Vonnegut, Kurt—Criticism and interpretation. 2. Vonnegut, Kurt—Knowledge—
United States. 3. United States—In literature. I. Title.
   PS3572.O5Z743 2009
   813'.54—dc22

                                                                    2009003440

This book was printed on Glatfelter Natures, a recycled paper with 30 percent postconsumer
waste content.

For Asa Pieratt, bibliographer at the clambake

CONTENTS

PREFACE

Kurt Vonnegut's America derives from what I was doing in the days following Kurt's death. Knowing that he'd suffered irrecoverable brain injuries in a fall three weeks previous and, after all measures to help him failed, that he'd been taken off life support a few days before, I received the news with a sense of grim inevitability. I'd been mourning for almost a month and knew his loss would be difficult to bear.

But then, within hours of the public announcement, everything came alive. Away from home—I was up in Madison, Wisconsin, doing research on Frank Lloyd Wright—I was hard to reach, but phone messages poured in. National Public Radio, a number of state public-radio networks, CBS News Radio in Los Angeles, the Jim Lehrer NewsHour, even the BBC: everyone wanted something on Kurt Vonnegut. And so I complied, giving what was asked, from thirty-second comments to hour-long discussions. *All Things Considered, To the Point, Nightwaves,* and many more—the whole roster, it seemed, of public broadcasting that usually figured in my life as background to the day's events. For now, Kurt Vonnegut was the event, and it brought his work to life for me in a way four decades of literary criticism hadn't.

The book at hand was begun right after the last of these radio shows and is written in the style I found comfortable for discussing Kurt's impact on his country. It is personal and critically informal yet rooted in the common dialogue Americans share, especially when considering national matters that touch their own lives. Millions of lives were indeed touched by Vonnegut's works, and it's in the voice I found so natural for *All Things Considered* and the other discussions in which I took part that this book is written.

Kurt had been expecting death, hoping for its release for some time, outspokenly since having lived longer than did his father. And so my book begins with a treatment of this sense of release, perhaps the last conscious thoughts he had as he toppled off his front steps there on East 48th Street before his head hit the pavement. It ends with a sense of Vonnegut uncaged, the drawing he left as his epitaph.

Preface

I'm not a computer person, but friends tell me that empty birdcage, door open, appeared in the Kurt Vonnegut Web site the day after he died. Maybe it's still up there now. Print-oriented folks can see it stamped on the hardcover edition of *Timequake,* the book that Kurt had declared would be his last novel, and that was. I'm glad he's free. But his influence is still with us, and that's what *Kurt Vonnegut's America* is about.

My thanks go to all those public-radio outlets that got me going on this project, to André Eckenrode for his helpfulness in tracking internet sources, to the readers who refereed this book for the University of South Carolina Press, and to the University of Northern Iowa, which has always been and probably always will be my sole source of support.

INTRODUCTION

Vonnegut Released

Kurt Vonnegut died late in the evening of April 11, 2007, at the age of eighty-four years and five months. Five months precisely—his birth date was November 11, 1922, Armistice Day, as it was called then, when there was only one world war to remember. It was a hallowed occasion throughout the 1920s and 1930s and into the 1940s, until a new world war would steal attention. At eleven minutes after the eleventh hour of the eleventh month of each year, schoolchildren paused from their lessons for a moment of silence. At work and at home, adults would do the same. As a veteran himself, a pacifist but nobly civic in his intent, Vonnegut recalled those ceremonies as subsequent decades effaced them, the event renamed Veterans Day and for a time having its celebration shifted to the closest Monday. It has since been restored to its proper date, which pleased him. Aged veterans of the First World War had told Vonnegut that in 1918, when at this precise minute the gunfire and explosions had suddenly stopped, the silence sounded like the voice of God. Throughout his own career as a writer, he'd tried to give voice to the sentiments behind such memories of an ideal America. And now the living presence of that voice had been silenced.

His last years, the first of this new century, had been difficult for him. After *Timequake* (1997), his fourteenth novel, itself a struggle to produce, he complained of being tired, of wishing to do no more work. After all, he'd labored on for two decades after conventional retirement age, trying to make things better for an age in which everything seemed to be going wrong. His novel in progress, the story of an old-fashioned comedian, never took satisfactory shape; what survives is its title, *If God Were Alive Today*. Henceforth people worrying about subsequent atrocities and abominations might use the same sad phrase about Kurt Vonnegut. He'd tried his hardest, but with a nightmare war in Iraq, unchecked global warming, and a sad deterioration in cultural civility, the tasked seemed almost too much.

As for himself, Kurt Vonnegut feared that he'd be forgotten, or at best regarded as a relic of the 1960s. Ironically his death proved how wrong he was. On the morning of April 12, 2007, *The Today Show's* Ann Curry announced his passing as a major news item. That evening on *NBC Nightly News,* Brian Williams treated it with the respect for the passing of a Melville or a Faulkner. The *CBS Evening News* gave the story of Kurt's death its last seven minutes, a time slot reserved since Walter Cronkite's days for the subject of deepest reflection. Of course, these newspeople had known the man, hosting him on their interview shows whenever he'd have a new novel to promote or be speaking out on an important current issue. They too were of the generation that had read him when they were young, part of the 1960s–70s generation that had propelled *Slaughterhouse-Five* (1969) to best-sellerdom and enshrined paperbacks of his earlier novels as classics.

But this was not all. That evening, Jon Stewart gave over part of *The Daily Show* to a clip of Kurt Vonnegut's appearance from late in 2005, and he ended the program on a rare serious note, saying that with this man's death, "The world today is a colder, emptier place." Sober stuff, especially for a younger generation the author feared was lost, or at least lost to his message. But the message was alive. In the even more outrageous *Colbert Report,* scheduled to ramp up Jon Stewart's irreverence to a higher, gratingly ridiculous level, host Stephen Colbert restricted his customary biting segue to just five words: "Welcome to the Monkey House!"

That's the title of Vonnegut's 1968 story collection, the satirical tone of which actually paved the way for today's sharper edge of sociopolitical comedy, be it Stewart's, Colbert's, or David Letterman's. Kurt Vonnegut had done the Letterman show in 2005 as well. Indeed he'd become famous all over again with a newly enthralled young audience, thanks to his recently written essays being collected and published as *A Man without a Country* (2005). Given quiet publication by a small press, it astounded everyone by rocketing to the *New York Times* best-seller list.

From *The Today Show* at 7:00 A.M. to *The Colbert Report* at 11:30 P.M., Kurt Vonnegut had been the major story of the day. Far from being forgotten or dismissed as depleted, he'd gone out under full sail.

The last book of his published in his lifetime is the right place to start in understanding both the life and work of Kurt Vonnegut. *A Man without a Country* is a strikingly contemporary work. Its concerns, from international politics and the environment to the nature of our country's leaders presently responsible for these matters, speak to the moment. Yet this very pertinence is based in its author's perspective, which from a man in his eighties is a long one, spanning at least six major eras in America's last one hundred years. For everything Vonnegut says about the events of 2000–2005, especially the troubling uncertainty of what's going on these days, there's a grounding or contextualization in something Vonnegut knows, something he's experienced and reflected on, and which offers a clue to making things better.

As a baseline for understanding the present, Vonnegut starts with his own childhood back home in Indiana. It surely was a simpler time, with the prosperity of the 1920s enjoyed in the company of a large, financially comfortable, reasonably happy family: father a prominent architect, mother a brewery heiress, older brother Bernard destined for doctoral study at the Massachusetts Institute of Technology and a career as an atmospheric physicist, older sister Alice gifted in the arts and receptive to little brother Kurt's appealing comedy. That's how he got attention, he recalls on this book's first page: breaking into otherwise inaccessible adult conversation by virtue of saying something funny. The first time was probably something he said by accident, he guesses. But, after witnessing such success, he began to refine his comic art and use it as much as he could.

Its first test was the second era he experienced, that of the Great Depression. No more prosperity. The Vonnegut family's economic decline was dramatic: no architectural commissions for the father (who became disinfatuated with the arts), no inheritance for his mother (because of her own father's remarriage), and no fancy private schooling for Kurt (such as Bernard and Alice had enjoyed). Sadly the Depression unhinged his mother, leading to years of rages fueled by barbiturates and alcohol, ending with death by her own hand. More happily the necessity of public schooling delighted young Kurt, giving him not only an excellent civic education but providing him with a democratic base of friends. As for comedy, where else could he learn vernacular jokes such as a "twerp" being someone who wedges a set of false teeth between his buttocks to bite the buttons off bus seats, where else but in a public high school?

As for the fearful instability America faced in these Depression years, the newly elected president, Franklin D. Roosevelt, counseled that there was nothing to fear but fear itself, but young Kurt Vonnegut had a better idea. "Humor is an almost physiological response to fear," he noted at the time and recalls on page three of *A Man without a Country*. Especially fear of death. That's why he savored the comedy of Stan Laurel and Oliver Hardy. He'd laugh his head off at their antics, tragic as many of them were. "These men are too sweet to survive in the world and are in terrible danger all the time," he notes. "They could be so easily killed" (4). Kurt Vonnegut himself could have been easily killed at age twenty-two, when as a prisoner of war interned in Germany he experienced the firebombing of Dresden, a raid that inflicted upwards of 135,000 deaths, the largest single-event massacre in European history. Here in *A Man without a Country*, sixty years later, he recalls a joke from that night in the underground slaughterhouse shelter, when during the worst of the bombing a fellow soldier ponders, in a warbling upper-class lady's voice as if commenting during a cold and rainy evening, "I wonder what the poor people are doing tonight?"

"Nobody laughed," Kurt observes, "but we were still all glad he said it. At least we were still alive! He proved it."

In this same opening essay Vonnegut gives his serious diagnosis of how humor works, something he talks about in interviews and codified in a previous nonfiction book, *Palm Sunday* (1981). Here the example is a question about the constituency of bird droppings; there the question concerns the high price of cream. Subject matter is not the point—it's the notion of being questioned that's important. Answering questions is hard, Vonnegut writes in *Palm Sunday*, even fearful as he notes now in *A Man without a Country*. Why so? Because our intelligence is at stake. It's hard work to think, and embarrassing if we get the answer wrong. So when the question is posed as to why the price of cream is so high, we freeze up a bit, not knowing why but assuming we should. Dumbfounded, we sit imprisoned in our tension until the speaker answers his or her own question: "Because the cows hate squatting over those little cartons." Relieved, we laugh—not because the line is sidesplittingly funny, but because the tension of being put on the spot has been released. There *is* no correct answer! We've been absolved, and that feels great!

Right here is the simple reason why Kurt Vonnegut's writing has not only pleased so many people, but made them feel better about life, horrible as life can sometimes be. His narratives are constructed like jokes, carefully setting a tension (just like a mousetrap) and timing it right so that just at the moment of greatest need (when the mouse reaches for the cheese) the trap is sprung. Like the mouse, we are put out of our misery, humanely so. The difference is that we are not mice scavenging for food but rather human beings looking for answers. In cases where there *are* valid answers, Vonnegut gives them. After all, he's been considered one of the most socially responsible writers of his generation. But where there are no answers, or where readers have been trying to fashion them when there's no need, he gently shows us how we've been wasting time and energy, worrying about nothing at all.

There's a postmodern literary and philosophical theory for what writers far more sophisticated than Kurt Vonnegut have done: deconstruction. Beginning in the 1960s, thinkers such as Jacques Derrida and others set and released the same type of mousetraps, taking concepts long accepted as basic and showing how completely fabricated they were. *Interrogating previously unquestioned assumptions* is the thumbnail definition of this method, and Vonnegut's genius was not just discovering it on his own, but voicing it in an accessible, commonly vernacular manner. *A Man without a Country* revels in this technique. A serious worry throughout the book is, for Vonnegut at least, the behavior of President George W. Bush. The author abhors his policies, domestic and international, but is able to play a neat little mousetrap joke on those who'd take his citation of Divine guidance seriously. "By his own admission," Vonnegut writes, the president "was smashed, or tiddley-poo, or four sheets to the wind a good deal of the time from when he was sixteen until he was forty. When he was forty-one, he says, Jesus appeared to him and made him knock off the sauce, stop gargling nose paint." With these comically slang terms for alcoholism reverberating in our ears, the author pauses, signaled by a paragraph break. Then comes Vonnegut's answer, in his classic single-sentence paragraph form: "Other drunks have seen pink elephants" (41).

On the other hand, there are things President Bush has done that Kurt Vonnegut takes with great seriousness, giving his readers an insightful answer where one is most desperately needed. By late in 2005, when *A Man without a Country* appeared, a majority of Americans had become uncomfortable with and even distressed by the war in Iraq, which had turned from its early and relatively painless (to Americans) success into a genuine nightmare, with hideous suffering on all sides. Agonizing over the war itself, Vonnegut turns to the soldiers, whose "morale, like so many lifeless bodies, is already shot to pieces." Why is morale a serious casualty, and why does it give readers a truly helpful answer to the dilemma of opposing the war while supporting our troops? Because Vonnegut, a combat veteran himself, can make a simple comparison, one that speaks volumes in just one short line: because "They are being treated, as I never was, like toys a rich kid got for Christmas" (72).

The comparison is invidious, but in a way that makes the author's satire appealing rather than revolting, ultimately comforting rather than alienating. For Vonnegut, George W. Bush is not a bloodthirsty murderer, as President Lyndon Johnson had been so ineptly characterized by humorless critics during the Vietnam War, another conflict the author had opposed. Instead the genius behind the Iraq War is shown to be the doings of a spoiled child, a son not of poor farmers but of a previous president of the United States, a wealthy one at that. Terrible as the results have been, the problem is familiar kids' stuff. And so solving it should be an easy matter, if we just start acting like Doctor Benjamin Spock.

What a relief!

The rhythms of Kurt Vonnegut's writings are those of jokes, but also of another popular form, journalism. The essays collected in *A Man without a Country* originally appeared on a semiregular basis in a magazine called *In These Times,* but the author learned the ropes as a journalist much earlier—in public high school, in fact. Shortridge High in Indianapolis boasted a daily student paper. Thrilled with this extracurricular work, young Kurt rose to the position of Tuesday editor. For his higher education, begun in 1940 at Cornell University in Ithaca, New York, where he'd been sent to study something "useful" (biochemistry, as opposed to anything in the arts that had so disappointed his father during the Great Depression), he gravitated away from studies and athletics to a similar post with Cornell's student daily, the *Sun.* Here he did hard news, producing a morning paper for not just campus but the entire city. In *Palm Sunday* he speaks with relish about the experience, obviously the most important of his college life:

> I was happiest here when I was all alone—and it was very late at night, and I was walking up the hill after having helped put the *Sun* to bed.
>
> All the other university people, teachers and students alike, were asleep. They had been playing games all day long with what was known about real life. They had been repeating famous arguments and experiments, and asking one another the sorts of hard questions real life would be asking by and by.
>
> We on the *Sun* were already in the midst of real life. By God, if we weren't! We had just designed and written and caused to be manufactured yet another morning newspaper for a highly intelligent American community of respectable size—yes, and not during the Harding administration, either, but during 1940, '41, and '42, with the Great Depression ending, and with World War Two well begun.
>
> I am an agnostic as some of you may have gleaned from my writings. But I have to tell you that, as I trudged up the hill so late at night and all alone, I knew that God Almighty approved of me. (66–67)

Serious journalism, to communicate, demands rhythms that will first spark a reader's interest, then sustain it, and (after not too long a process) satisfy it.

For more than fifty years Kurt Vonnegut's writing, whether in fiction or expository prose, exploited these qualities. To mimic plain, direct speech (which newspaper readers expected), he'd write short sentences, sometimes of just one word. Paragraphs, as in a newspaper, were short as well, sometimes just a single line. And, above all, journalism requires honesty. Again from *Palm Sunday* comes the author's assessment of his relative success: "I myself find that I trust my own writing most, and others seem to trust it most, too, when I sound most like a person from Indianapolis, which is what I am." Where is such language first found in written form? In the local newspaper, the *Indianapolis Times,* where young Kurt worked summers as a high school student drafting ad copy to be read by other teenagers. It was not to be found in traditional literature, where the alternative was "the one most vehemently recommended by teachers [that] has no doubt been pressed upon you, as well: that I write like cultivated Englishmen of a century or more ago" (79). In all of Vonnegut's work, no teacher is singled out as a mentor. That role is reserved for Phoebe Hurty, dedicatee of *Breakfast of Champions* (1973) and a figure described in its preface as the hometown editor who not only taught Kurt his trade but instilled his manner of honesty, even at the risk of being impolite.

Such impoliteness runs through all of Vonnegut's work and is a favorite technique in the essays of *A Man without a Country.* The author does not mean to be offensive per se, and certainly not hurtful—he's said many times that he never wants to make a person feel like something the cat's dragged in. Manners themselves, with their sense of common courtesy, are important to him, but only when sincere. It's an insult to decency when politeness is used to obfuscate the truth. His own way of being impolite is strategic: to upset preconceptions, to mix in the surprising, to *defamiliarize,* as the theorists put it, which means to refreshen the reader's view, sweeping away the cobwebs of assumptions that dull one's vision. Take global warming, an issue that by 2005 would seem to have been written and talked to death. "Don't spoil the party," he says, acknowledging the fact that our civilization has carried on so irresponsibly, "but here's the truth: We have squandered our planet's resources, including air and water, as though there were no tomorrow, so now there isn't going to be one." Pause, paragraph break. "So there goes the Junior Prom, but that's not the half of it" (45).

Junior Prom? Talk about a rudely jarring disruption of an otherwise sober thought. But sobriety has done little to curb global warming. Perhaps reminding readers that their immature, adolescent attitudes and behavior will be accountable just might do some good.

Four years after his own Junior Prom and before he could finish college, Kurt Vonnegut was inducted into the U.S. Army. Detailed as an advance infantry scout, he was captured at the Battle of the Bulge, imprisoned in Dresden, and at war's end repatriated by the Russians—but not before surviving the firebombing of Dresden, the most horrific aerial assault of the European war and controversial to this day. Back home, he married his childhood sweetheart, Jane Cox (met in dancing class), and wondered if he could write about his Dresden experience. He couldn't. Not so much because of authorship deficiencies, but because readers in 1945 weren't ready for it. Instead he'd spend the rest of the 1940s studying anthropology at the University of Chicago and covering events for the reporter pool known as the City News Bureau. After two years he moved to a position as publicist for General Electric's Research Laboratory in Schenectady, New York, where his brother Bernard (who'd arranged the job) was working on the concept of cloud seeding to produce rain. Unhappy with such work, Kurt literally wrote his way out of it from his new home on Cape Cod; family-magazine short stories provided a living through the 1950s. But still no Dresden book. As it happened, America was scarcely ready for the five novels he published between 1952 and 1965. None of them was a commercial success or even had commercial viability. With the magazine markets drying up, he turned to fill-in jobs, from writing advertising copy to teaching, for a time at a school for troubled children near his home in West Barnstable, Massachusetts, and later for two years (1965–67) at the University of Iowa Writers' Workshop.

By the late 1960s the country was ready for Kurt Vonnegut's Dresden book, and in 1969 he published it as *Slaughterhouse-Five*. Ostensibly about World War II, it is really about the author's writing of the book, with much attention to its protagonist's life twenty-some years after Dresden. What was happening twenty years after? Vietnam. As Vonnegut recalls in *A Man without a Country*, he opposed the war, as eventually did most of his fellow citizens:

> But I think the Vietnam War freed me and other writers, because it made our leadership and our motives seem so scruffy and essentially stupid. We could finally talk about something bad that we did to the worst people imaginable, the Nazis. And what I saw, what I had to report, made war look so ugly. You know, the truth can be really powerful stuff. You're not expecting it. (20)

Slaughterhouse-Five was not only a huge best seller, but propelled its author into the cultural and sociopolitical limelight. His comments were noted as lead news items in *Time* magazine. Major universities and organizations asked for speeches, and leading magazines printed them. Fame was not fleeting. Indeed, after quietly building up a twenty-year canon of largely unnoticed work, Vonnegut had reams of material ready for paperback reprinting, satisfying a readership that suddenly wanted more of him. At two- to three-year intervals throughout the 1970s and 1980s, new best sellers followed, both novels and collections of essays.

By the 1990s Kurt Vonnegut was tired. But not too tired to produce *Timequake* (1997), a virtual autobiography of a novel that made its own making more interesting than anything else. And in the last months of 2005, just a year and a half before his death, *A Man without a Country* was embraced by a new generation of readers making their own discovery of this man and his writing. As such, it is a good introduction to Vonnegut. Everything's there, from his Indiana childhood to the wars in Europe, Vietnam, and Iraq. It even gives an intimate portrait of the man, more than eighty years old, going about his daily business, such as this new generation likes to do with its webcams and blogs. In an eight-page essay titled "I Have Been Called a Luddite," Kurt takes the excuse of why he doesn't use a computer to follow himself around his neighborhood, in which carrying a typewritten manuscript to the mailbox involves buying an envelope one place, buying a stamp at another, and spending a luxurious amount of time savoring the familiar world he moves through.

Isn't he wasting time? His wife chides him that he's not a poor man—he could easily have a box of envelopes on hand and plenty of stamps, much less own the world's best home computer. But that would cheat him of his stroll around the 'hood, the pleasure of which he'd been working on for days at the typewriter. There, putting words on the page, he's tried his best to save the world, doing all he can to make things a bit more tolerable, even though it will all die anyway. So it goes. Now, however, it's time for life.

"Electronic communities build nothing," he concludes, finally answering the reader's question. "You wind up with nothing. We are dancing animals. How beautiful it is to get up and go out and do something. We are here on Earth to fart around. Don't let anybody tell you any different" (61–62).

It would be remiss to let this portrait of Kurt Vonnegut in life close without telling what I myself learned about the man over the past thirty-five years that I was his critic and he was my friend. Critic. Friend. That can sound facile. Of substance to Kurt's imagination, I was also a character in his fiction, one of a group of people from his real life that he invites to the fictional clambake that concludes his novel *Timequake*. Some of his friends were mine, too—Loree Rackstraw, Bob Weide, Asa Pieratt, Peter Reed—and many of us who'd last met as characters on page 206 were back together via phone calls in the week before his death. We'd been warned it was coming. Three weeks previous, we were told, Kurt had been sitting on the front steps of his New York City townhouse, enjoying a cigarette. Standing up to return inside, he'd lost his balance and fallen, hitting his head. A neighbor saw the accident and called for help, but any real help was too late: there had been massive brain damage, the frontal lobe destroyed, and he never regained consciousness.

For nearly a month he held on. Doctors made sure he was not suffering, but recovery was impossible. *So it goes* had been Kurt's mantra for death in *Slaughterhouse-Five,* but none of us said or even thought that now. Instead, for an epitaph Kurt had one ready since 1968. There, in the preface to his story collection *Welcome to the Monkey House,* he'd cited lines from his brother and sister that seemed the best summation of his fiction. Bernard had written after bringing home a new baby: "Here I am, cleaning shit off practically everything." Alice, dying of cancer, had left these final words: "No pain."

For the next month, as we five characters in search of an author grieved, the media showed its own respect by treating Kurt's death as a monumental passing. I've described how the commercial networks and cable shows responded. Within an hour of the first announcement a producer from Jim Lehrer's *News Hour* show was on the phone, followed by people from *All Things Considered, To the Point,* and any number of state public networks, plus CBS News Radio in Los Angeles. Calls came in with the day's progress across time zones, ending with the BBC Radio Three show *Night Waves.* I did as many of these as possible, most of them just standing there speaking into the phone, but scheduling a feed to London from my university's broadcast studio to be done once I got home. Peter Reed did the National Public Radio special. And so on.

Since our first notice that Kurt was about to become unstuck in time, his life and works have become a newly vitalized topic. It certainly tuned me up for what I am writing now, and I trust it will be different from anything on the author and his work I've done before. As Jon Stewart said, with the loss of this person, the world is indeed a colder, emptier place. But any thought of the man and his books lightens us up again, if only for a moment.

Although I'd been reading his books since student days in 1966, I didn't become a Vonnegut scholar until 1970, when I was asked to teach a Twentieth Century Novel course. The course went well. I did an essay on *Mother Night* and *Cat's Cradle* for *Critique's* spring 1971 issue and, with the course in mind, started working with John Somer on an anthology, *Innovative Fiction* (1972). Its publisher was Dell, paving the way for our next book, *The Vonnegut Statement* (1973), with the firm's premier hardcover line, Seymour Lawrence /

Delacorte Press. As Lawrence was Kurt's own publisher—most famously for the book contract that produced *Slaughterhouse-Five* as the author's first best seller and reinforced his reputation for the ages by bringing his previously neglected work back into print in hardcover, quality paperback, and mass paperback editions—the door was opened for my own professional friendship with Vonnegut. Searching through library sources, I'd located scores of uncollected stories and feature essays the man had written over the past twenty years, a period during which he'd taken any assignment possible as a way of keeping the wolf at bay. Should they be collected now? Lawrence said yes, while Kurt Vonnegut said no, fearing that the stories had been passed over once (when assembling *Welcome to the Monkey House* in 1968) because of various weaknesses. Well, how about doing just the essays? I made a valiant plea for their worth, showing how the author's manner of dealing with fact would help readers understand his experiments in fiction. Vonnegut agreed, and the book appeared as *Wampeters, Foma & Granfalloons: Opinions* (1974). Prefacing it was the author's bemused characterization of the event, a deliberately mixed metaphor in which his works were archaeological artifacts while John Somer and I were winsomely practicing "therapeutic vivisection."

But he did call us "Two nice young college professors" who meant well, so the preface was friendly. As was its challenge: that not even the most hideous torture conceived could force him to reveal the whereabouts of three or four pieces we'd not found. A few pages later he revealed why: at least one of them was an embarrassingly sentimental piece about literary influences imparted to him as a child by the family's African American cook. What a tease, and a harmless one, as he'd already admitted the presumed weakness. It took another dozen years, and Asa Pieratt's help, to find two of these essays. But not the remembrance of those happy hours spent with Ida Young and her old-timey storybook, *More Heart Throbs.* Vonnegut did add that he wished he had access to that volume now. Within months readers had inundated him with copies.

Wampeters, Foma & Granfalloons, as I knew it would be, was a best seller, going through scores of paperback printings and persisting as an active title today. It did clarify the author's larger method, but also gave readers two new aspects to consider: the man's personality (as a basis for so much of his writing style), and his stature as a public spokesperson for important social and political issues. From now on, Vonnegut saved what he wrote, compiling *Palm Sunday* as an autobiographical collage in 1981 and undertaking a more thorough recrafting of his next decade's nonfiction for *Fates Worth Than Death* (1991). And where would we be without *A Man without a Country,* the 2005 book that let Kurt Vonnegut's career close at new heights?

So from 1972 onward this man was my professional friend. But in 1972 there was someone besides Seymour Lawrence who showed interest in my critical work. This was the year I began living every young professor's dream, moving at age twenty-eight to an up-and-coming new university that provided not just a senior position but convenient teaching and abundant resources for research. The best resource turned out to be a person, my new colleague Loree Rackstraw. Her office was next to mine, so we saw each other often. But had she been far across campus, we still would have become friends, because her own closest friend on earth was Kurt Vonnegut.

I'd known, of course, that he'd taught for two years (1965–1967) at the University of Iowa, mentoring young fictionists in the Writers' Workshop. But I'd dismissed it as one of his fill-in jobs, taken in desperation when his story markets had collapsed and his novels were not selling. Shouldn't I have guessed that someone like Kurt Vonnegut would have produced dozens of brilliant students? Later on I'd come across several, including John Irving. But here, right next door, was the first one, from his first creative-writing class in Iowa City.

Loree's other mentor that year was Richard Yates. Like Kurt he was a man more than a thousand miles from home, improvising his way through a job he wasn't trained to do, and wondering if his literary career would ever amount to anything. Also, like Kurt, he was an infantry veteran of World War II, from the same campaign. Quite naturally the two became close friends, a friendship that would last a lifetime. Part of the professionalism of the Writers' Workshop is its social scene; as much or more education takes place out of class than in. Given Iowa City's reputation as the Athens of the Midwest, a virtual Paris or Florence (or Greenwich Village!) in the cornfields, students and faculty banded together, sharing a life not just in class but in the town's abundant cafés, coffee shops, and bars. Plus Loree had two young children in tow, reminding Kurt of his own brood back on Cape Cod. Here was company, the extended family based on mutual needs and interests that he would always insist on as a necessity of life. There were famous writers on hand, including (that year) Nelson Algren and José Donoso. But Kurt and Dick were the unknowns or little-knowns, working at the bottom of rank and salary (instructors at sixty-eight hundred dollars per year, less than a quarter of what professors earned). And so while Algren and Donoso lived the better life, Kurt, Dick Yates, and Loree and her friends found solace in simpler places such as the Airliner, Murphy's Pub, and the Hamburg Inn.

A year later, M.F.A. degree in hand, Loree signed on to teach at the University of Northern Iowa ninety miles north in Cedar Falls. Having just been upgraded from a teachers college, UNI was eager to act the part. Guest lectures plus poetry and fiction readings from visiting stars were encouraged. Kurt Vonnegut was far from being a celebrity, but he was a professional, and so for one hundred dollars he drove up Highway 218 for an evening's talk. A small classroom was adequate for his thoroughly respectable audience of forty or so. He donated his fee to the Quakers. His talk was as insightful and amusing as any there had heard. Three years later, in 1969, Granville Hicks would review the surprising best seller *Slaughterhouse-Five* with a similar speech in mind, one he'd heard Vonnegut give at Notre Dame University. The man had a vernacular appeal akin to Mark Twain's, Hicks observed, a personal presence that the novel was able to capture. Years later, when I reminded Kurt of this review, he told me how "People do seem to like my work best when they've heard me speak first."

Now it was 1972: Kurt was world famous (commanding speaking fees of ten thousand dollars and more), and I was newly arrived in Cedar Falls. He'd told Loree I was coming. Our first conversation lasted the better part of an afternoon, and it has continued off and on for more than thirty-five years.

I had much to learn. How important Kurt's two years in Iowa City had been, his first experience of living in a community of writers—and in a state that valued the arts so highly as to fund an idealistic institution such as the workshop. How sympathetic he was to anyone who'd work hard at an art, whether it be Nelson Algren, sleeping off a hangover in the student union, or the female impersonators entertaining at a nightclub to which some students had taken their teacher as a joke. Above all, the importance of his work. Didn't he feel neglected, overlooked, a professional failure exiled to teach in the middle of nowhere? "Not at all," Loree told me. "Even then he had a clear idea that he was doing something important, that sooner or later the world would take heed."

Thanks to Loree Rackstraw, Kurt Vonnegut became my personal friend. Everything you've heard about him is true: the late-night phone calls, the prompt response to letters, the occasional self-doubts, and most of all the delight in a good laugh. "Cheers," he'd say after just a minute or two on the phone, or write at the end of a quick, to-the-point letter. During my time he made half a dozen visits to Cedar Falls, usually for lectures (by then to more than a thousand in our largest auditorium), sometimes just to visit friends (Robley Wilson, another of his students, also taught in our department and edited the *North American Review,* to which Kurt sometimes gave material). I visited him in New York several times but usually stayed in touch by telephone and mail.

On the phone, in a letter, or across the table, Kurt was always very closely aware of his partner in conversation. He expressed himself with an exquisite sense of timing, a timing determined by the dynamics of dialogue taking place. I remember well one evening on Loree's sun porch, with a small group of us lounging on the comfortable sofa and chairs, talking about anything and everything. Kurt, Loree, myself, Bob Weide, Peter Reed—anyone for a clambake? (It was probably evenings like these that prompted the scene with all of us in *Timequake*.) Others were there as well, including Loree's daughter from her second marriage, Deedee, now college age. Well, twenty years old (a charmingly innocent twenty; Deedee looked not a day over fourteen) was a big stretch from us oldsters, and when Bob told a slightly off-color joke, he at once felt embarrassed and struggled to apologize. "Good grief," Kurt interrupted, feigning concern, "don't say *fuck* in front of the B-A-B-Y." More than just timed right, his line took Bob off the hook and kept everyone feeling just fine. In practical terms, like a good infantryman, he'd taken a bullet for his buddy, one he knew he could bear. But we all were better for it.

This same sense of timing, of structuring a situation for best impact, characterized the more serious things Kurt would say. Over lunch at the Mona Lisa Restaurant, around the corner on Second Avenue from his New York townhouse, he was helping me complete a timeline Seymour Lawrence had requested for the next book I was doing, *Vonnegut in America* (1977). Much of what Kurt told me about his childhood and young adult years was new, so I was happily taking notes. As much to give myself a break as to avoid restating the obvious, when we got to 1945, I mentioned that we probably didn't have to say more about that.

"No," Kurt agreed, and began a serious string of remarks I presumed were in confirmation of this.

"You know," he continued, "the raid didn't end the war one day earlier, didn't save one life, not of an American soldier, Russian soldier, or concentration camp inmate."

While I nodded in agreement, he took another spoonful of spaghetti and motioned me to do the same. Were we done with this point?

No. He had more to say.

"Only one person benefitted from the bombing of Dresden," he added, looking at me over his food.

"One person?" I asked, rising to the bait.

"Yes," he said. "Me." Raising his napkin to wipe a spot of red sauce from his mustache, he made his point. "I got three dollars for every man, woman, and child killed there."

Six months later, he made this same point in a *Paris Review* interview, and in time it became part of his preface to a new edition of *Slaughterhouse-Five*. Doubtlessly he had been trying out the line on others as well, but that's my point: Kurt was always sensitive to how his material was being received, how his listeners were reacting. His lectures were the same. Time and again I'd marvel at how he'd work an audience, giving more of something when it seemed to be succeeding, dropping a topic the moment it threatened to go over like a lead balloon. Even in simple conversation, if he could make someone laugh, he felt he'd succeeded. And what did he succeed at? Providing the excuse to laugh himself, which he'd do so vigorously as to induce fits of coughing.

But besides all the information and all the jokes, Kurt was, quite simply, a good friend. I was pretty young and raw when I met him. Indeed I was just a couple years older than his son, and so the natural style was for him to act fatherly. In 1976 I was nominated for a professorship at the State University of New York at Albany. That's where Kurt's brother, Bernard, was teaching, having retired from General Electric. So during my campus visit I walked over to the physics building, introduced myself, and asked his advice about conditions at the school and in the state. But I'd written Kurt, too, and on return found one of the most helpful letters I'd ever receive.

Yes, Kurt had lived in the Schenectady-Albany-Troy area for two years (1948–50), but all he'd liked about it was being able to live next door to his brother. He'd phoned Bernard to get an update about the university, learned I'd just dropped by myself, and so knew all that. Then he got serious.

"If you move east, you'll find you become a floater," he counseled. At his present age, thirty years after leaving the Midwest, he felt he was mostly helium. He then mentioned how I was valued and needed at the university in Cedar Falls, and he marveled at what a nourishing situation that must be. Recalling that I drove an old Mercedes-Benz sports car and played in a blues band on weekends, he said I obviously had a sense of style.

"Here is the most stylish and useful thing to do," he concluded. "Iowa is a better place than New York. Stay where you are."

I've never regretted that I did.

Kurt wanted me to be happy. "You must know that," he added in a phone message thirty years later, responding to some photos I'd sent him of the little farm my wife and I were fixing up way out in the country. He'd met Julie only half a year after I myself had met her. Just twenty, she was brave enough to tolerate a trip to New York City (her first east) and meet "my friends." For ten days it was quite a whirl: book parties at the Strand (Donald Barthelme), deli lunches on Sixth Avenue (Jerzy Kosinski), openings at the Gotham Book Mart and elsewhere, all filled with any number of imposing New Yorkers. With Kurt it was different. Quiet. Gentle. Unassuming. Smiles rather than laughs. "He twinkles," she told me afterwards, comfortable in New York for the first time. Kurt had made her feel that way. She'd brought a book for him to sign, and the way he did it was part of his secret, making himself less the famous author than a schoolyard friend. "For my pal Julie Huffman," the inscription read, for that's what she'd become during the visit.

On one of Kurt's own visits to our home, when our kids were little, our daughter Nina (just six) helped with dinner, bravely serving him a second helping of onion soup. A quarter century later, well into her legal career in Chicago, she was walking past a bookstore on Michigan Avenue when she noticed a book signing taking place inside. It was Kurt Vonnegut! Approaching the table, she identified herself as my daughter.

"Little Nina!" Kurt exclaimed. "And how's dear Dad?"

More than thirty-five years later, our children had grown into adults. I replaced the blues band with a minor-league baseball team (which equally amused Kurt), went from there to a fascination with World War II air-combat narratives (he was no fan of these), and stayed happy in Iowa. During this time I watched myself hit ages that had been benchmarks in my friend's life and observed him growing even older. I was there the first time he began urging people to pause and take notice of pleasant moments. Like passing an open window and hearing a piano being played beautifully, or sitting on a shady lawn on a hot summer day, enjoying the breeze and a glass of fresh lemonade.

"Isn't this nice!" Kurt encouraged us to say, just as his uncle Alex had said to him and others back home in Indiana.

I saw his worry, too, even his fatigue that kept him from working on a last novel or helping Bob Weide do more filming for what promised to be the best author documentary ever made.

But he bounced back. He'd get angry for sure, such as when the government had taken our country to war in Iraq. Yet, at his maddest, he could still make a joke about poor W, his vice president, and first secretary of state. A rude one he felt was excusable for *A Man without a Country:* "The last thing I ever wanted was to be alive when the three most powerful people on the whole planet would be named Bush, Dick, and Colon" (40).

"But now I am eighty-two," he added. "Thanks a lot, you dirty rats." He'd amused himself by threatening to sue the makers of Pall Mall cigarettes for welching on their promise, stated on every package he opened, to kill him.

Well, the last one did. May he rest in peace.

1

VONNEGUT'S 1950s

Human Structures

Kurt Vonnegut's debut as a writer of fiction came on February 11, 1950, when *Collier's*, one of the great family oriented weekly magazines of the era, published his story "Report on the Barnhouse Effect." But as the key date in his literary career, October 28, 1949, looms more important. For it was then, with the acceptance from *Collier's* in hand and with assurances from the editors there that two more were likely to be taken as well, that the new author wrote his father—not just with the news, but with a solemn promise to continue in this field, no matter what.

On that day in 1949, Kurt was just two weeks short of his twenty-seventh birthday, a husband and father himself, and established in a career that promised to take him smoothly into the postwar world of corporate success. As a publicist for General Electric's Research Laboratory, where "Progress Is Our Most Important Product," he was on the cutting edge of his culture, not just watching new technologies be devised but promoting their embrace by the culture at large. His own brother, Bernard, was one of the lab's star scientists. But even at twenty-seven, Kurt was still the baby of the family, and, at this important juncture of his life, he thought it important to check in back home.

Home was Indianapolis, Indiana, where he'd been raised at the core of a large extended family. But in these postwar years it was becoming dispersed. His father's architectural practice had been ruined by the Great Depression, his mother had become so disturbed by the changing nature of the times that she took her own life, his older brother and sister were out east (like him), and the once-prosperous hardware business his uncles had run was on its way to being run out of business by foreign competition. For a solid midwesterner who'd loved the sense of family, community, and civic order Indianapolis had provided for his childhood, his move to GE in 1948 had opened up a brave new world indeed. In England, where even more startling social, political, economic, and cultural transitions were taking place, George Orwell had reversed that year's last two digits for his own novelist view of how things were changing, *1984.* Working for GE in Schenectady, New York, Kurt Vonnegut found his own vision was a troublesome one as well—troublesome, that is, if he stayed within the corporate structure that promised to dominate the new era.

He desperately wanted out, and, with the acceptance from *Collier's,* it looked like he had found a way. That's why he was writing his father: not just to merit the old man's faith, but to make a promise to himself, bonded with someone who'd helped create him.

He'd just sold his first story, but he had done something more than just that. At noon yesterday, on lunch break from GE, he had put the entire payment for it in the bank. He'd do the same for the next two likely to be accepted, and he hoped to do the same for the two after that. This would give him a savings account equal to a year's salary at the publicity office, where he'd not been comfortable at all. But there was more news, and an even more serious promise.

Made in 1949, in a letter reproduced in the author's autobiographical collage published in 1991, *Fates Worse Than Death,* it involves the nature of the rest of his life. With the income from five short stories banked to live on, "I will then quit this goddamn nightmare job, and never take another one so long as I live, so help me God." With a paragraph break for emphasis, he says what every parent hopes for his or her child: "I'm happier than I've been for a good many years" (26).

Kurt has this letter on hand in 1991 because his father not only saved it, but enshrined it as workroom plaque, varnishing the page to a board decorated with a quotation from Shakespeare's *The Merchant of Venice:* "An oath, an oath, I have an oath in Heaven: / Shall I lay perjury on my soul?" Since his father's death in 1957, it had hung in his own workroom, a space dedicated to writing fiction and personal essays. This, not Orwell's world of 1984, would be Kurt Vonnegut's.

Some of that work involved writing his own novel, *Player Piano* (1952), to accompany George Orwell's *1984* and Aldous Huxley's *Brave New World* as classics of dystopian fiction. In 1959 he published an even more apparently futuristic novel, *The Sirens of Titan.* But both books are really about the present, about Kurt Vonnegut's 1950s, a decade he was doing all he could to prevent the development of the nightmare world Orwell and Huxley had foreseen. They are best read in the company of the short stories he'd continued doing for *Collier's* and soon for its senior competitor, the *Saturday Evening Post.*

Five a year for these venues would equal the annual salary he'd been earning in the corporate world, but now he was doing it on his own terms, drafting works that suggested how progress for its own sake wasn't a very good cultural product at all. As a husband of a sensitive, conscientious woman and as the parent of no less than six children, living in the middle-class community of West Barnstable, Massachusetts, he damn well knew it! His fiction was now in close touch with neither utopians nor dystopians, technocrats nor idealistic dreamers. Instead it spoke the language, fed the interests, and answered the concerns of people like himself.

Kurt Vonnegut stayed a member of that economic class for the next twenty years, averaging no more than five stories per year, which gave him (as he liked to recall) the salary a high-school cafeteria manager could earn. (Until 1969, when *Slaughterhouse-Five* became his first best seller, the novels rarely earned more than their small advances, taken as stopgaps when no stories were being accepted.) How close were these stories to his daily life? Although his own autobiographical collages either focus on the present or gravitate to his experiences in youth, Kurt's wife and son each wrote memoirs of that period. In 1987, Jane, recently remarried as Jane Vonnegut Yarmolinsky, had her heirs publish *Angels without Wings: A Courageous Family's Courageous Triumph over Tragedy* (she herself had died of cancer in December the previous year). The tragedy involved the deaths of Kurt's sister and brother-in-law within days of each other, while the triumph was achieved by Kurt and Jane's immediate adoption of their three orphaned nephews. But both terms also reverberate among the details of living on the meager earnings of an unfamous author and coping with the pressures of his creative life. Wouldn't suffering all that drive someone crazy? It did have an impact on the eldest, Mark, Kurt and Jane's first child, who later on as a young man aged just twenty-two underwent a full-fledged schizophrenic breakdown. He not only recovered, but wrote a book about it published in 1975, *The Eden Express*. With ample material about his childhood, it serves as another key account of Kurt Vonnegut's America taking shape in the 1950s.

Two other texts frame the author's 1950s: his preface to *Welcome to the Monkey House* (1968) and his introduction to *Bagombo Snuff Box: Uncollected Short Fiction* (1999). The first volume, published before he was famous but with the support of an initial three-book contract from Seymour Lawrence that within a year would take him there, comprises Kurt's selection of what he then considered his best short fiction. The second, published toward the end of his career, adds the culls—material that in 1974 I'd thought good enough to be included in *Wampeters, Foma & Granfalloons* (Kurt demurred and had to be argued into reprinting even his essays) and that a quarter century later Peter Reed, having written an excellent study of all Vonnegut's short fiction, persuaded him should be saved, albeit as "uncollected."

As scholars would say, the canon for Kurt Vonnegut's 1950s is complete: not just the published stories from that period and the two novels, but commentary on their lives at the time from all parts of the family, including father, mother, and son. Having this context clarified is essential, even in terms of literary art, as during these years the author was generating his material from who he was and where he lived.

"Where I Live" is the first piece in *Welcome to the Monkey House,* technically an essay but written in the new manner of personal journalism that used the techniques of fiction—character, imagery, development by dialogue, and the like—in order to present a more personally credible, imaginatively rich picture of the subject. By the late 1950s and early 1960s, a cadre of self-styled "New Journalists" had appeared, including Dan Wakefield, Joan Didion, Tom Wolfe, Gay Talese, and others. Vonnegut's essay, first published as "You've Never Been to Barnstable?" in a slick monthly called *Venture—Traveler's World,* is indicative of the new forms and markets he'd sought after his short story outlets, *Collier's* and the *Post,* began cutting back on fiction before eventually shutting down completely. But its manner is one with his stories, and, as a portrait of his life in the 1950s, while making a middle-class living among other tradespeople and professionals in this thoroughly conventional Massachusetts community, it sets the tone for his older *Post* and *Collier's* stories that follow. How it squares with his own prefatory accounts and memoirs from his wife and son seals the case that the 1950s being presented in *Welcome to the Monkey House* and *Bagombo Snuff Box* were Kurt Vonnegut's own.

Its format is a traditional one, a device favored by Mark Twain and other nineteenth-century writers: a stranger comes to town and has to be educated to the community's ways. This is precisely what Kurt, Jane, and son Mark experienced in 1951 after pulling up stakes in Schenectady and moving to the cape. Provincetown, any writer's first choice, had proved too arty for what Vonnegut had in mind for his home life and the type of fiction he wanted to write. In "Where I Live," the incomer is an encyclopedia salesman, eager to bring the town's library (and its citizenry) up to date. Instead he finds a social group set comfortably in its ways. True, these ways are quaintly idiosyncratic and in some cases downright stupid. Consider the town's fishermen, who for years refused to believe that tuna were any good to eat, instead calling them "horse mackerel" and throwing them back into the bay, chopped up as a warning to other horse mackerel. But the community, unfashionable as it is, has prospered in a way highly valued by the author: there's a role for everyone, from the eccentric yacht-clubbers to the Episcopalian minister who made his special contribution as a church gardener. Set as it is near the root of Cape Cod, West Barnstable is the diametric opposite of Provincetown, and a good place where Kurt could raise a family and write his fiction. Why so? Despite being a gateway to holiday-land, it made a quiet point of existing for itself, not for passersby.

As a coda to his tale, the author adds that the library finally has an up-to-date encyclopedia, but so far there have been no improvements in children's school grades or the level of adult conversation. Apparently those grades and the small talk had been good enough all along.

Right here is the structure of more than half the stories Kurt Vonnegut would write and publish in the 1950s. Individuals, couples (dating or married), families, and communities would be tempted away from their core values. For a time they'd be enthralled by illusions, be it the perfect social personality, sudden wealth, designer lifestyles, or utopian technology. That would be the action's first movement, akin to West Barnstable's exposure to the encyclopedia salesman. Then, in each story's second act (as it were), they'd be disappointed in not getting what the illusions had promised. Sometimes they'd even look weak or stupid, as with the first piece's fishermen who chopped up expensive tuna and tossed them into the water. But don't fear: their simple standards would triumph in the end, proving that their own original ways were best. "Poor Little Rich Town," "Custom-Made Bride," "The Foster Portfolio," "Who Am I This Time?"—again and again Vonnegut would exploit this formula, riffing many variations as a jazz musician might on the familiar pattern of a twelve-bar blues. The permutations were endless, truly infinite, because their structure was based on a fundamental essence of human social behavior.

Kurt knew the formula from life. He'd tried deviating from it in his career as a corporate publicist for the General Electric Research Laboratory. But what he'd seen promised no happiness. Progress for its own sake eroded core values, simple values based on the most central structures of human society. If asked, he could have quoted chapter and verse from the latest findings in anthropology, which he'd spent two years studying on his postwar G.I. Bill benefits at the University of Chicago. During the time he was there (1945–1947), the department's leading scholar, Dr. Robert Redfield, was developing his thesis of the folk society, demonstrating how groups of about two hundred people could not only survive self-sufficiently but do so in a pleasing manner, keeping every one happy because there was a job for each member, a way every person could feel that he or she was of use.

Not surprisingly, a character in Kurt Vonnegut's first novel, *Player Piano,* holds a master's degree in anthropology. But he's a Protestant minister as well, indicative of how, for his larger works of the 1950s, the author would seek his own sense of structure in both areas of human activity, the social and the religious. A religion had been the focus of Kurt's own intended master's thesis at Chicago: the Ghost Dance Society of Plains Indians in the 1890s. These Native Americans had used a form of religion to organize their revolt against the encroaching white civilization, and as a student of anthropology Kurt wanted to use them as the variable in his study of what it took to form a revolutionary community (his control group was the world of Cubist painters in early-twentieth-century Paris). And so revolution in art was a matter of Vonnegut's structural interest as well. But taking the issue this far, by comparing primitive and civilized societies, was at the time considered too radical, and so was Kurt's next idea, comparing the plot lines of folktales and modern magazine stories. Both were rejected by his professors. As an aspiring author, Vonnegut learned his lesson well. For what would become his family's bread and butter, the fifty-some stories he'd publish during the 1950s for the great family magazines of the time, he stuck to conservative structures, ones that affirmed well-being of the community for what it was. It would be in his novels *Player Piano* (written as the decade was beginning) and *The Sirens of Titan* (done at end of the 1950s) that toyed with the revolutionary aspects, respectively, social and religious, of structure.

If the social climate at General Electric in the late 1940s was anything like the futuristic world portrayed in *Player Piano,* it's easy to see why Kurt Vonnegut wanted out. There's science and technology aplenty in this novel, but what's important are the human relations, of people trying to make their way among the altered structures of this new-style world. Supposedly, as in all utopias, the changes have been for the better. Here in this new era, following a presumed third world war, all the drudgeries of human labor have been effaced. Ingenious machines do everything, providing a decent standard of living for everyone. No one except the engineers has to work, and their work involves more company politics than intellectual labor. There's the first problem: their work as such is meaningless, with no more substance to it than the abstraction of General Electric's slogan, which presented progress as its own goal. As for the goods provided to the people, they are adequate. But lives themselves are empty: with no real work to do, no one can have a sense of being useful, of being needed for anything. Vonnegut knows people believe that life must have purpose. When it seems not to, they invent it. His persistent hope is that they do it harmlessly, on the level of art and play. The danger is when "purpose" is construed as a God-given absolute, as happens when religions take themselves too seriously. *The Sirens of Titan* demonstrates just this. But religion is also a force in *Player Piano*. That's why the revolution's leader is not just an anthropologist but a minister. And what he opposes is the way technology has become its own reason for being, its own justification of life—in other words, its own religion.

This is the structure Kurt Vonnegut's novel hopes to reveal. Supporting it are two classic narrative devices, ones the author often cited as the basics for an infinite number of stories. A stranger comes to town. A man and a woman seek each other and either do or do not find happiness. In *Player Piano* the stranger is a minor functionary, a simple observer (from the outside) of the action. He's a stranger indeed, the Shah of Bratpuhr, visiting the factory on a State Department tour. His questions sound quaint, phrased as they are in his native language with colorful words such as *khabu* (where), *siki* (what), and *akka sahn* (why). But by shading these terms with an exotic hue, Vonnegut lets them pierce the official smugness that would obscure the true nature of life in this utopia, which the Shah's disarming comments reveal to be much more dystopian than the government and technology experts can admit.

The Shah of Bratpuhr's words sound like nonsense syllables, because they are. But his nonsense clears away the official version of sense in this technocratic society, showing how it has given itself over to a worship of the machines. The government and company spokespersons are speechless, but not the machines. They themselves have plenty to say, such as "Furrazz-ow-ow-ow-ow-ow-ak! ting! Furr-azz-ow-ow," "Vaaaaaaa-zuzip! Vaaaaaaa-zuzip!," and "Aw-grumph! tonka-tonka. Aw-grump! tonka-tonka" (10) and so forth, a virtual musical suite. At a company party, fireworks are set off to similar sounds. On a drill field, a company of soldiers is given commands in a similar panoply of barked half-syllables. It's all mechanical, just like the automatic washer at the home of the man and woman seeking happiness with each other, Dr. Paul Proteus and his wife, Anita. Their washing machine comments on its own work cycle: "Urdle-urdle-urdle," "Urdle-urdle-ur dull," and "Znick. Bazz-wap!," ending with a conclusive "Azzzzzzzzzzzzzzz. Froomph!" (96). The couple, trying to make sense of life with a happy marriage, can of course speak, and they do. But most often their conversations end with a mechanical mantra of "I love you, Paul," and "I love you, too, Anita," the rote repetition of which means little more than the "urdles" of their automatic washer.

Is there any meaning at all? Were he a simple dystopian, Vonnegut could easily say no. But nihilism is not the American way, certainly not the way of a beleaguered middle class struggling to find its way in the new postwar reality.

Consider the longest line in all the Shah of Bratpuhr's dialogue, the most complete statement in this novel from the religious leader of six million people, whose comments have deflated the pretenses put before him. "*Puku pala koko, puku ebo koko, nibo aki koko,*" he intones. A secret of Eastern wisdom, the key to solving all these problems in the West? No, just a set of instructions to the barber, translated as "a little off the sides, a little off the back, and leave the top alone" (174–75).

A line, when translated, that could be spoken by any *Saturday Evening Post* character of the time! In *The Sirens of Titan,* one such person appears, described as such, sporting a tell-tale dab of shaving cream behind his ear, and bearing the name of one of Kurt Vonnegut's recurrent family-magazine characters, bandmaster George M. Helmholtz (86). It's a joke, of course, but not a morbidly meaningless one. Instead the strange new world that at times seems so fearful proves to be utterly familiar, even in the person of the mysterious stranger venturing in.

Does this constitute sentimentalism, akin to what the *Post* was putting on its covers as paintings by Norman Rockwell? Only if, as when viewing a Rockwell canvas, one stops at the surface. The drawback with great public art is that the public may, if it wishes, leave the work with simply a first-glance impression. That impression will not be wrong but misses the chance for a deeper sense of completion, of resolution. Consider the famous Rockwell depiction of a bad moment during a Chicago Cubs baseball game. Framed are the dugout bench and the first row of fans sitting just above. Two lines of people are reacting to what has surely been a terrible play; there's not a happy face in the bunch. Stopping right there, a point can be made: the hapless Cubbies have failed again, and the ballplayers are as disgusted as spectators. But if one stays with the picture for a few more moments, a larger narrative evolves. Moving down the bench, one distinguishes ranges in age (from the older manager to the younger players to the adolescent batboy) and expression (from disgust to disbelief, from anger to resignation), all of which interact with the various fans and their differing expressions above. Only at the end of this process does it dawn on the viewer that he or she can feel any of these ways, too—without even having seen the play! And there's the resolution: we don't even need a view of the playing field to know that once again the loveable losers have performed in character, that for some teams there's a winsomely sad predictability to defeat, that the Cubs *and* their fans seem fated to suffer forever.

Player Piano accomplishes much the same, and in a remarkably similar manner. Far from being an exotic science-fiction tale or mind-bending experiment in cybernetics, it is fashioned much the same as the author's *Saturday*

Evening Post and *Collier's* stories. There "post-war" means after World War II rather than a prototypical World War III, but in making adjustments to new technologies, economies, politics, and demographics Vonnegut's lesson is the same. However the "ies" and "ics" change, human beings still remain the same. As he'd discovered in his ahead-of-the-times research in anthropology, Plains Indians in 1890 had much the same motivations as Cubist painters in Paris just a decade later. People are people. It's all one world.

Hence the suitability of this novel's resolution. After staging a successful revolt, the workers—led by Dr. Paul Proteus, who has seen inside the system his father helped build, and Reverend James J. Lasher, whose own view is both anthropological and religious—unwind by tinkering, helplessly fascinated by the challenge of reassembling and repairing the machines they've just destroyed. People need something to do. Life demands purpose. The danger is inventing too dominating a one. Or one that subverts structures necessary for human happiness.

In *Player Piano* the structures are clear. Technological revolution has subverted the human need for purpose. But even the counterrevolution, led by Proteus and Lasher, succeeds only temporarily—the machines are destroyed, but human fascination will rebuild them. Not until 1985, with his novel *Galápagos,* will Vonnegut go so far as to suggest genetic devolution as a solution; preceding that extreme move is the reformulation of religion in 1959 with *The Sirens of Titan.*

Society's structure of human purpose is complemented by Kurt Vonnegut's understanding of the family. Paul and Anita hope that "I love you / I love you, too" will provide a refuge (as Howard and Helga's "nation of two" hopes to suffice in the author's third novel, *Mother Night,* in 1961). But as Vonnegut would say throughout the 1980s, when he was most comfortable in his role of public spokesmanship, a husband and wife, just the two of them, are unable to supply a world to each other. That's why couples are motivated to have children and why children have not just siblings but grandparents, aunts, uncles, and cousins. Indeed the happily extended family is the author's ideal, one lived by him in his Indianapolis childhood and suggested, with some whimsy, as an artifice in his novel *Slapstick* (1976). In between, during his own family life on Cape Cod in the 1950s, his sense of parenting and familial duty came into play when the Vonnegut clan's own structure was threatened to be torn apart.

This story is told by Kurt's first wife in *Angels without Wings.* Because it is a true story, she changes the names to protect the innocent, as it were. Kurt becomes "Carl," son Mark is "Matt," daughters Edie and Nanny are "Amy" and "Nelly." Why not? By the time Jane Cox Vonnegut wrote this book, she was Jane Vonnegut Yarmolinsky, remarried in the 1980s as Kurt had been in the 1970s. But *Angels without Wings* is about the time when they were all together, living as conventional a 1950s life as any American family could, given that its income provider was a fiction writer. But even that role is subsumed in the rhythms of family life, the symphony of which Kurt Vonnegut had found easier to conduct here in West Barnstable than as a research-lab publicist in Schenectady. Jane describes the Monday morning of September 15, 1958, as starting like any other, the kids off to school, she settling down to pay some bills, her husband at work in his study:

> I could tell by the rhythm of the typewriter that the work was going well. It was about time. Ever since the previous February, when he had finally gotten an advance on the book he had been working on for two years before that, Carl had been struggling to finish it. March, April, and May had been fairly productive months, our spirits buoyed by the advance and by the sale of a short story earlier in the winter. But the distractions of the summer had brought work almost to a halt. Weekend after weekend, vacationing friends and relatives and friends of relatives would show up—a well-known hazard of living on the Cape—and many of them wouldn't go home on Sunday night, not seeming to understand that the house was also a place where a man had to make a living, for God's sake. The kids' noisy comings and goings added to the tumult. It was an old story. We had lived with it for years. It's what we talked about at cocktail parties on the Cape in the summer.
>
> The time had gone pleasantly enough, actually. Which, of course, was the problem. Pleasure at that house was always getting in the way of the serious business of life. It was a sparkling mix of fun and high anxiety laced with neurosis. When you added the stress of reality—like not having enough money to pay bills—who could stand it? (5)

Sound like a Kurt Vonnegut story from *Collier's* or the *Post*? A family center, with corresponding centripetal and centrifugal forces, a man and woman seeking happiness as work draws the husband to his typewriter, only to be pulled away by kids flying out the doors and windows. Strangers come to town (those friends of relatives), but there's an extended family as well, friends *and* relatives. A fluctuation, too, such as Kurt had studied in folktales at Chicago and worked into his own stories of the 1950s, fun and anxiety mixed with neurosis. Indeed, who could stand it? Paragraph break. "Carl and I could, that was who," Jane concludes, mirroring the endings of so many of her husband's short stories.

The challenge to this carefully balanced order comes from two deaths in the family: not just the sadly anticipated loss of Kurt's sister, Alice, from cancer, but—a mere day and a half earlier—the death of her husband, quite improbably as a passenger perishing on the only commuter train in history to plunge off an opened drawbridge, but no less final for that. To make it worse, Alice—whom the family had prayed could die in peace—overheard a nurse mention the accident, giving her terrifying worries for the welfare of their children.

Like a hero and heroine in the *Saturday Evening Post,* Norman Rockwell cover and all, Kurt and Jane at once adopted Alice's kids—three boys, aged just a year or two older than their own. And, like any family in a *Post* story, they struggled. If it was hard supporting a family of five on this bread-winner's income (virtually any middle-class family's story of the times, making their way through the economic recessions of 1957 and 1959), how on earth could it be done for eight? Especially when the three new kids were traumatized by their parents' deaths and enduring a distant move into an entirely new home. Well, that's what makes it a story worthy of publication, in *Collier's* and the *Post* or in *Angels without Wings.*

It was not all angelic. Kurt and Jane were unable to adopt their fourth nephew, because he was just a baby and other relatives insisted he needed closer attention. That was a blow. And the six cousins did not always get along smoothly—not because of personal difficulties, but because the structure of a traditional nuclear family was being stretched almost out of shape. And of course there was the special nature of the father's profession, hard enough anyway but especially difficult as a free-lancer, nervously living from single sale to sale. In *The Eden Express,* son Mark Vonnegut recalls how by Christmas 1970, the family's last holiday together, things were coming apart:

> There we were, my family, my blood. Cousin brother Jim, twenty-five, tormentor of my late childhood and adolescence, my replacement as eldest son, two-time college flunk-out, no particular direction, a couple thousand dollars in photographic equipment, his inheritance, shrinking fast. Cousin brother Steve, twenty-two, three months older than I, Most Popular Barnstable High School Class of '65, B.A. Dartmouth, teaching English in Barnstable High, his alma mater, hating every minute of it, planning to quit but without the faintest idea of what he was going to do next. Cousin brother Tiger [proper name, Kurt] with a year to go at U. Mass. No real plans but with a pilot's instructor license and reasonable prospects, undoubtedly in the best shape of anyone there. They were my

father's sister's sons. We had adopted them when their parents died when I was eleven. It was a real bitch at first but things worked out.

Sister Edie, twenty, two-time college drop-out, no direction, hooked up with and apparently unable to get free from Brad, a second-rate Charlie Manson. Sister Nanny, fifteen, very unhappy about school and lots of other things. My father having difficulties adjusting to superstardom, not wanting to be a writer any more, very restless, not very happy about anything. My mother going through menopausal stuff, wondering what the hell to do with her life with the kids all grown and the marriage not in the greatest of shape. And myself, twenty-two, B.A. in religion, fed up with do-gooder work in Boston, no plans and less hope for what the future held. (58)

Certainly no *Saturday Evening Post* story! But by then the magazine was defunct, like *Collier's*, both of them a faint memory of what the 1950s had been. The 1960s were a rough decade for Kurt Vonnegut, with the 1970s not much better, first a lack of markets and then a surfeit of them testing his strength as a writer. But Mark's Christmas-card snapshot shows how the times had changed. Old structures had been challenged and overturned, and new ones were not yet in place. Putting them in place was just the job his father was supposed to be doing, and in time he'd get it done. But for now things were in flux. As the young man points out so many times, no one, not even the best of them, had a clear sense of direction.

Mark's college degree was in religion, where a search for purpose was foremost. His father had looked into religion, too, examining its structure in *The Sirens of Titan*. Here, rather than seeking a purpose *in* religion, Kurt examines the purpose *of* religion, much as he'd done with issues of family and work in *Player Piano*. To do so, he takes a broad view of matters. What he produces is no more a strictly religious novel than a space novel (or work of science fiction). Rather he draws on another of the oldest narrative structures known—the business of two separate actions in progress, separate until they cross—to have religion interact with outer space. On Earth an eccentric person of old wealth, given the classically upper Hudson Valley name of Winston Niles Rumfoord, seeks to regenerate human awareness by introducing a new style of religion, a style he has discovered on a privately financed space mission during which he has not only experienced but become trapped in a new dimension of existence. Does this sound far-fetched, the stuff of shabby space opera? Well, there's plenty of space opera in *The Sirens of Titan*—Rumfoord's dog, who has been with him for this ride into the new dimension, is called Kazak, the Hound of Space. And it gets much worse than that. Vonnegut is obviously mocking the form, a proto-postmodern way of drawing attention to his act of fabrication and discouraging any suspension of disbelief.

But there are links to a credibly real world and to serious sociopolitical issues. For his characterization of Rumfoord, Vonnegut obviously has Franklin Delano Roosevelt in mind. Roosevelt, like Rumfoord, was old money from the Hudson River Valley, but he was also president for most of the author's adolescence and young manhood—for thirteen years of Vonnegut's thirty-seven years of age to date. Roosevelt, like Rumfoord, always had his dog (Fala) at hand. The two men's speech is typified by their "glottal Groton tenor" (20), making their greetings sound like songs. Unlike science-fiction writers (who by necessity focus on issues and ideas), Vonnegut had established himself as a master of description, especially when creating characters. Even a minor functionary such as *Player Piano*'s State Department host, the slickly smooth Dr. Ewing J. Halyard, is more than just "a heavy, florid, urbane gentleman of forty." Vonnegut can do a lot better than that, and he wants his readers to think more deeply about the type, and so he continues: "He wore a sandy mustache, a colored shirt, a boutonniere, and a waistcoat contrasting with his dark suit, and wore them with such poise that one was sure he'd just come from a distinguished company where everyone dressed in this manner." Very good— Vonnegut not only dresses him up, but has the dressing spark a reaction among observers. But there's more, more about Halyard and more about ourselves: "The fact was that only Doctor Halyard did. And he got away with it beautifully" (17).

Slick, smooth, and snazzily effective—and crooked as a snake! Because of his care with the language in creating people, Vonnegut is able to make Winston Niles Rumfoord more than just a cardboard cutout for science-fiction thematics. In terms of what readers know of America—Kurt Vonnegut's America, and theirs—Rumfoord is a familiar type, an aristocrat of merit and intelligence whose deep feeling for his fellow humankind motivates him to seek a better solution for happiness. For FDR, that reordering of priorities was the New Deal, a reinvention of the national economy with government taking a leading role in improving its citizens' lives. To accomplish much the same, albeit in a post-Rooseveltian world in which beneficent economics is not enough, Rumfoord offers not new government but a new religion, the Church of God the Utterly Indifferent.

Here is where the paths of Earthling life and intergalactic space travel come together. As readers follow the contemporaneous action of Rumfoord's design for a better life on Earth unfolding, they also can view it from a higher perspective, which is that of their planet being observed telescopically by a stranded flying-saucer pilot on Titan, the largest moon of Saturn. The pilot, a Tralfamadorian named Salo, has been sent on a trailblazing mission across the universe, bearing a secret message undisclosed even to himself. When his spacecraft breaks down on Titan, unable to receive communications from home, he is restricted to watching messages in the Tralfamadorian alphabet take shape on the third planet of the solar system visible above him. These messages are in regard to his mechanical problem and cover the time during which his home base is working to get him going again.

In one of his earliest examples of super-succinct paragraphing (later a hallmark of his mature style). Vonnegut ticks off the messages Salo gets. Four paragraphs, four sentences, four brief messages written on the face of Earth so that they could be telescopically visible from the largest moon of Saturn.

The communications are written in Tralfamadorian, but they translate easily enough. *Be patient, we haven't forgotten you,* reads the first; to an Earthling, however, this message is more commonly recognizable as the Great Wall of China. *We are doing the best we can,* Salo's home base tells him an epoch later, this time spelling out the words by means of the Golden House of the Roman Emperor Nero. Well, Salo's an understanding sort and is pleased to read, more than a thousand Earth-years later, that *You will be on your way before you know it.* (Of course he will, having been sufficiently patient to watch the Kremlin's walls be constructed in Moscow so as to spell out this encouragement.) Finally, as doings on Earth settle down sufficiently to build (and place hopes in) the Palace of the League of Nations, Salo gets a last-minute update: *Pack up your things and be ready to leave on short notice* (271–72).

Short notice indeed: a third of a century! But that's in Earthling time, one of the illusions this Tralfamadorian perspective destroys. Not to mention any sense of human purpose, struggle, and suffering. Think of it, as readers are encouraged to do, as a technique that would make the shortest of Vonnegut novels large enough to fill a lifetime of contemplation: think of not just the size of that wall in China but of the bones of dead workers mixed into its bonding; think not just of the grandeur, glory, and accomplishments of Rome, but of the sufferings wrought by Nero; of the immense story of Russia, of the carnage of World War I and the hapless hopes for peace that followed. All for what? To send messages to a stranded flying-saucer pilot, waiting with the same exasperation a stranded motorist might feel when the wrecker is delayed. And flatly banal messages at that! The Great Wall of China, the Kremlin, Woodrow Wilson's dream for a better world, all reduced to empty happy-face post-it notes.

So much for intuitions of human purpose, at least from the human point of view. What did World War I accomplish, a war still present in human memory in 1959, when this novel was published? Have your bags packed for departure on a moment's notice. Sure. Just like "the check is in the mail."

As for what the Tralfamadorians have been up to, the secret message turns out to be just this: "Greetings." Its vacuity is too much even for Salo, who during his long wait has not only learned much human history but become close friends with an Earthling or two. The futility of it literally tears him apart.

To flesh out his novel with human action, Vonnegut devises a second plot that interweaves with both Rumfoord's doings on Earth and Salo's on Titan the story of Malachi Constant's involvement with the plans of both. New money rather than old, garish rather than subtle, Constant is enough of a contrast to Rumfoord to qualify *The Sirens of Titan* as a novel of manners—as is his relationship in space with Salo, which is one of true friendship. When he dies, happily and peacefully, which is the best Kurt Vonnegut can promise any of us, it is with an understanding that "somebody up there" likes him (319). The phrase, as commonly vernacular as any of the messages to Salo, customarily means God. But from the scene itself readers know that it's Salo and from the novel's larger action that all sense of purpose is a fabrication, completely unrelated to any deity, beneficent or malevolent. Things just happen, and they might as well be the doings of flying-saucer repair as anything else.

That's what Rumfoord's Church of God the Utterly Indifferent teaches: that there is no ruling Absolute that will make sense of life, that any attempt to discover Purpose per se will yield a ridiculous space opera. Like Roosevelt, Rumfoord knows that to unite the people in adhering to this new understanding, there's nothing like a war to pull everyone together. Hence the book's staged invasion from Mars. Like World War II, it works. But the question, as always, remains what will people do afterwards.

How could the author of such a sophisticated novel, or even of a science-fiction novel (as some would have it), be producing, at this very same time, story after story for *Collier's* and the *Post*? Critics have long separated the two activities, and Vonnegut himself habitually excused the short fiction as having been done to buy time for writing his novels. But, as with *Player Piano,* the structures that generate this author's short fiction and long are compatible. Human strivings, disappointments, and resolutions are much the same in *The Sirens of Titan* and benefit from similar manneristic descriptions of characters. In chapter 3 Vonnegut borrows a major character from several of his stories, the high school bandmaster who helps solve any number of adolescent problems. To fill out the scene, he brings in the school's algebra teacher as well. Just because here the two happen to be secret agents from Mars does not obscure the fact that for this theme, as well as all others in *The Sirens of Titan,* Vonnegut is dressing it out in familiar terms and reminding readers that they already have the tools for making sense of things, if they just look back to their basic values. The setting is also familiar, a small cocktail lounge (known as the Hear Ye Room) in the Tudor-styled Wilburhampton Hotel, located in one of the shabbier areas of Los Angeles:

> In the Hear Ye Room were three people—a bartender and two customers. The two were a thin woman and a fat man—both seemingly old. Nobody in the Wilburhampton had seen them before, but it already seemed as though they had been sitting in the Hear Ye Room for years. Their protective coloration was perfect, for they looked half-timbered and broken-backed and thatched and little-windowed, too.
>
> They claimed to be pensioned-off teachers from the same high school in the Middle West. The fat man introduced himself as George M. Helmholtz, a former bandmaster. The thin woman introduced herself as Roberta Wiley, a former teacher of algebra.
>
> They had obviously discovered the consolations of alcohol and cynicism late in life. They never ordered the same drink twice, were avid to know what was in this bottle and what was in that one—to know what a golden dawn punch was, and a Helen Twelvetrees, and a *plui d'or*, and a merry widow fizz.
>
> The bartender knew they weren't alcoholics. He was familiar with the type, and loved the type: they were simply two *Saturday Evening Post* characters at the end of the road. (86–87)

Here's the answer to the novel's outer-space and new theology problematics, right in the common manners of the American 1950s, familiar from any page of *Collier's* or the *Post*—or from a look anyone could take into their local bar, with its tritely comfortable decor, its loveably shabby characters (outfitted in the same style!), and its banal but effective drinks. In every *Post* story where George M. Helmholtz takes a hand, matters have turned out OK. So they probably will here.

Don't take it all so seriously, the author is telling his readers, whether they be readers of religious speculation or science-fiction thematics. Consider the novel's fanciest device, the trans-Galactic phenomenon known as the Chrono-Synclastic Infundibula. Where a self-serious SF author (or even a cheap hack) might show off his or her technological brilliance by offering a complex definition, Kurt Vonnegut goes to a much simpler source, *A Child's Cyclopedia of Wonders and Things to Do.* Its definition is no less precise for being clear and helpful, right down to the notion that *infundibulum* means "funnel." But to rub it in, Vonnegut lets his quoted source add, "If you don't know what a funnel is, get Mommy to show you one" (15).

Problems of the universe are problems of the local cocktail lounge and just as likely to receive a much better solution. But the cocktail lounge *does* help us get by, as do so many comforts devised by people living sensibly within their culture—*within their own folk societies,* as a younger Kurt Vonnegut had seen demonstrated by his anthropology professors at the University of Chicago in the immediately postwar years. As Americans adjusted to the new postwar realities—new politics, new economics, new demographics, even new art and music (make that *of course* new art and music)—short stories and novels, especially in a commonly accessible form, helped get people settled: hence Vonnegut's work in *Collier's* and the *Saturday Evening Post,* and in a book-club selection such as *Player Piano* and a paperback original (rack size for drugstores and bus stations) such as *The Sirens of Titan.*

Kurt's preface to *Welcome to the Monkey House* and introduction to *Bagombo Snuff Box* confirm this orientation. For the former he was taking advantage of the first truly beneficial contract he'd ever had to gather what he considered redeemable from his work in a market now gone belly-up, the great family weeklies that had flourished between 1900 and 1950 and during this last decade had struggled to a finish, at least keeping Vonnegut and his family afloat. In the latter he writes as a famous novelist—one of the most famous in American literary history—who must account for what he did in his first decade as professional writer, a decade in which he had to "face the audience of strangers" (as he'd warn his students at the University of Iowa Writers' Workshop they had to do) with fiction both accessible and worthwhile, something that made them feel better about their daily life even as they spent a half hour of it as they read his short story.

"I have been a writer since 1949," Kurt says in the 1968 preface. "I am self-taught. I have no theories about writing that might help others. When I write I simply become what I seemingly must become" (xiii). After giving a quick sketch of his hometown (Indianapolis) and heritage (civic-conscious German-American), he describes his brother, eight years older, and his sister, dead from cancer, and mentions how two statements from them sum up his work: "cleaning shit off practically everything" and "no pain" (xiii–xiv). What he is, his family was; and what it all adds up to is his fiction. Having been accused (by the *New Yorker*) of having produced nothing more than "a series of narcissistic giggles," he takes the joke and rolls with it, inviting the reader to picture him "as the White Rock girl, kneeling on a boulder in a nightgown, either looking for minnows or adoring her own reflection" (xv).

And that's it. Take it or leave it. Plenty had left it; in 1968 Kurt Vonnegut was not yet famous. In a year, thanks to *Slaughterhouse-Five,* he would be, a sudden onslaught of attention that unnerved him and an influx of great wealth that struck him as a cruel joke, given that his family, which he'd worked so hard, even desperately, to support was now raised and departed. Thanks to heavy promotion by the book's publisher, Seymour Lawrence, Vonnegut's name was brought to the attention of critics and book-review editors, so that when *Slaughterhouse-Five* came to them next year, they'd have an awareness that the author was not a neophyte but a veteran of twenty years' sales to the slicks, an honorable enough profession to working journalists tasked with producing a newspaper's review section or writing commentary for the mass market. Indeed Seymour Lawrence had discovered Kurt Vonnegut by virtue of one of the man's own pieces of working journalism, a review of *The Random House Dictionary* published in the *New York Times Book Review* for October 30, 1966. It appears in *Welcome to the Monkey House* as "New Dictionary," and insiders can note why it may have struck Lawrence's eye: as a young man he'd worked for publisher Bennett Cerf, who is teased here. But the broader view is more helpful, which is that Seymour Lawrence had noticed the writer's Mark Twain–like appeal, an infectious use of the vernacular for bringing down abstractions and theoretics to a practical level. And also for having great fun with practically nothing! How on earth does one review a new dictionary? Of course, you can see if it has included any dirty words. But even the book's deep seriousness, its reason for existing, can be made both funny and insightful, made insightful *by means of* the fun.

Take the issue of prescriptive versus descriptive linguistics. Anyone reading the *Times Book Review* would already know, or could figure out from the terms themselves, that the former means how people should talk (according to the rules of grammar and syntax), whereas the latter is how people actually do converse. Sound interesting? Only if it's going to be on the final exam. So leave it. But here's how Kurt Vonnegut, still an unknown in 1966, put the matter: "Prescriptive, as nearly as I could tell, was like an honest cop, and descriptive was like a boozed-up war buddy from Mobile, Ala." (108). At least one reader, Seymour Lawrence, a powerful publisher with his own line at the Delacorte Press division of Dell Publishing, took it, and the rest is literary history.

From that stature achieved in literary history, Kurt Vonnegut writes his 1999 introduction to *Bagombo Snuff Box,* the uncollected short stories from the 1950s that scholar Peter Reed had talked him into saving. "I myself hadn't saved one scrap of paper from that part of my life," Kurt says at the opening. "I didn't think it would amount to a hill of beans. All I wanted to do was support a family" (1). This is an important issue for the author, one that he drew further attention to when promoting the book on Michael Feldman's National Public Radio show, *Whad'Ya Know?* (October 2, 1999). Feldman, of course, received Vonnegut as a major author, famous for novels that had stretched the limits of innovation. Why, he asked, had Kurt written these apparently traditional pieces?

"Because I had to support my God-damn family," Vonnegut replied, bantering the line back and forth with Feldman throughout the interview, delighting the audience, and, in true Lenny Bruce fashion, breaking up the jazz musicians in the band.

Much of this introduction is devoted to what Vonnegut recalls as the great power of short stories—a power depleted at the end of the 1950s by the competition of television. He cites the great classics, and he describes the rise and fall of the great family weeklies that were once fat with stories and advertising. Interesting to note, he says the ads could be as stimulating as the fiction, simply because readers had to engage themselves with the magazine—so unlike just leaning back and turning on the TV. What personalizes all this history and theory is the story-within-a-story concocted for the introduction. Kurt calls it "our little domestic playlet" (5), in which Mother welcomes her teenaged son home from high school with a newly arrived copy of the *Saturday Evening Post;* he starts reading it and comes alive with its stimuli to the imagination, and—after all the usual disappointments of a day in school wash away—feels better. A few hours later Dad comes home, tired and vexed as well. Young Kurt directs him to the story he himself has just finished, giving him the warmed-up easy chair for a comfortable reading experience. Soon Dad feels better, too.

Television ended all this—for the magazines, which lost their advertising, and for readers, whose attention was now lulled rather than stirred. What this meant for Kurt Vonnegut was that short stories became harder and harder to sell, forcing him into such bridging quasi-employments as selling Saab automobiles, at the time virtually unmarketable to Americans, a story as hilarious as anything he'd write for the *Post*. Retelling it in 1999 made him feel better than he surely did in the 1950s, struggling to keep his family afloat. Knowing how by all this hard work Kurt finally succeeded, we cheer him along. It makes us feel part of the action, as the author goes on to say in conclusion, regarding the proper effect of a well-written story: "It makes the reader feel, even though he or she doesn't know it, as though he or she is eavesdropping on a fascinating conversation between two people at the next table, say, in a restaurant" (11).

One more point should be added, and that's the manner in which those overheard conversations in Kurt Vonnegut's stories become so accessible. It's because the language being spoken is the reader's own, the common vernacular of the great American middle class. Prescriptive linguistics? "An honest cop." Descriptive linguistics? "A boozed-up war buddy from Mobile, Alabama."

Kurt Vonnegut's last short story for the *Saturday Evening Post* was written in 1963, but never appeared there, though it is included in *Welcome to the Monkey House*. "The Hyannis Port Story" signals not only the end of Kurt Vonnegut's 1950s, but his transition to the 1960s, for what else was the presidency of John F. Kennedy? That's the story's subject, a new era being described in terms from the previous one that manage to make the innovation understandable.

All the hallmarks of Vonnegut's family magazine fiction are here, including the narrator from North Crawford, New Hampshire (a mythical small town much like West Barnstable, but without the readerly distraction of being located on Cape Cod) and his simple, familiar occupation (in this case selling and installing storm windows and screens). It's 1963, and the latest wrinkle in America's popular culture is the Kennedy phenomenon, a radically new take on both politics and lifestyles. At the moment, that style is running up against a possible counterrevolution, the candidacy of his likely opponent in the next election, Senator Barry Goldwater. It's a local debate over Goldwater that, by virtue of an amusing confusion, lands the narrator a job in Hyannis Port, "practically in the front yard of President Kennedy's summer home" (133). The customer is a preposterously mannered old-money conservative named Commodore William Rumfoord (there's that aristocratic name again), "Commodore" for his honorary rank at the yacht club. Rumfoord is not only a Goldwater supporter, but despises the Kennedy clan with a vengeance steeped in a century of social history.

Even before he gets to the Commodore's home, the narrator lets readers see the provocation, because the road into Hyannis is peppered with examples of Kennedy-mania, including "the *Presidential Motor Inn*, the *First Family Waffle Shop*, the *PT-109 Cocktail Lounge*, and a miniature golf course called the *New Frontier*" (71). Well, before taking on his installation job, the narrator needs lunch and so opts into the Kennedy craze at stage two, hoping to get a waffle. But the menu tells him it's not that easy, because all the items are named after the Kennedy family and associates. "A waffle with strawberries and cream was a *Jackie*," he notes, unsurprised. "A waffle with a scoop of ice cream was a *Caroline*" (readers can appreciate the cuteness, the sweetness of it all—they are still participating in the action). But then things get seriously weird, because, as the narrator notes, "They even had a waffle named *Arthur Schlesinger, Jr.*" That's too much for Vonnegut's readers, so the ridiculousness stops there. But what about lunch, a necessity for both plot and survival? "I had a thing called a *Teddy*" the tradesman reveals, letting it remain mercifully undescribed, accompanied by his own refamilarization of the entire scene, "a cup of *Joe*" (137).

A cup of Joe is the sole survivor from the 1950s and several decades preceding, but it gets the narrator (and us readers) through the story's first set of challenges. And what are those challenges? *Signs*. As literary theorists were just beginning to suggest, signs for things could be something quite apart from the things themselves that they describe. *Descriptions are their own reality*, deconstructionists such as Jacques Derrida and Gilles Deleuze had just begun arguing, helping to establish the new cultural understanding now called postmodernism. In "The Hyannis Port Story," Kurt Vonnegut was making that same argument, too, in his own vernacular terms. How else to explain all this Kennedy hysteria? And what about the contrary attitude of Commodore Rumfoord, whose home, right next door to President Kennedy's, is outfitted with a huge sign of its own: a portrait of Barry Goldwater, with bicycle reflectors for eyes and floodlit with blinkers.

"A man who sells storm windows can never be really sure about what class he belongs to," the narrator admits, having taken a paragraphed pause after encountering the Goldwater sign, "especially if he installs the windows, too" (137). But as he goes about his work, trying to keep to himself, the man can't help but notice how the Commodore's own world of signs, once stable, has been knocked awry by the Kennedys' new descriptions. A yachting harbor gone from sail to motors, a social climate in which poor Irish immigrants can rise to wealth and power, the futility of having named his son Robert Taft Rumfoord when the Republican party would be turning to the former Democrat Dwight D. Eisenhower instead—all this is disappointing indeed. But what the narrator's presence reveals is that the Commodore's greatest disappointment is in having nothing to do. When he learns this, as the value of work is being quietly demonstrated by the narrator, he comes to terms with the world, newly described as it is.

As such, this would be a simply sentimental ending. But Kurt Vonnegut has more. The Commodore turns off his sign, realizing how mean he's been to insult his neighbor. Does this mean his participation in the semiological world of postmodernism is over, too? Not at all. Because that evening, as the Commodore, his wife, and the narrator are relaxing on the veranda, enjoying the fruits of a job well done, a voice calls up to them. It is, as the story notes, that of "the President of the United States" (144), asking that the lights be turned back on.

Dumfounded, Rumfoord wonders why.

Were the Commodore's sign systems still operating as such, President Kennedy's first reason would have enraged him: Soviet premier Khrushchev's son-in-law is visiting and would like to see it. But the real reason is more familiar, the stuff of neighbors and neighborhoods and welcoming landmarks everywhere. Could the lights please be left on?, the President asks. "That way," he explains, "I can find my way home" (145).

Thus Kurt Vonnegut makes his transition from the 1950s to the 1960s. The *Post* soon died (as a family weekly), and postmodernism flourished (not just as a theory but as an index to an entire cultural transformation), but this new world could be understood by a simple readjustment of a few terms from the old.

"The Hyannis Port Story" was set in galleys and ready to run in a late 1963 issue of the *Saturday Evening Post* when the president's assassination caused it to be cancelled. It did appear in 1968 as part of *Welcome to the Monkey House*, squarely within a newer age when assassinations had become hideously more common. But in 1971, when assembling the anthology *Innovative Fiction*, all I knew was that the piece had been collected with no previous attribution. As I'd already been dealing with major authors on bibliographical matters— Donald Barthelme, Jerzy Kosinski, Ronald Sukenick, and such—I guessed I could write Kurt Vonnegut and ask him.

We'd yet to have any contact; that wouldn't come until a year later. For now, all I had was an address in *Who's Who:* Scudder's Lane, West Barnstable, Massachusetts. So I wrote, asking about the provenance of "The Hyannis Port Story" and whether my own list of uncollected works had any gaps.

Jane Vonnegut answered. Her husband "was away," she noted. In a few months Kurt's prefatory materials to his play, *Happy Birthday, Wanda June* (1971), would reveal why and where: to New York City, where he was starting a new life apart from his wife and family home. The reasons he gave for it were much the same as son Mark would detail in the Christmas Eve scene from *The Eden Express,* including pressures of fame and the emptiness of a house which all the children, now raised, had left. But back on Cape Cod, Jane was still doing wifely duty, generously answering my letter with a typewritten list of stories I'd missed. Plus a full account of the Kennedy story's history. Her husband was gone, but his files were still there—abandoned, as he'd say in *Bagombo Snuff Box,* as such entertainments were meant to last "about as long as individual lightning bugs" (2). But in 1971 Jane had them, and she was sharing them with me.

It's no wonder that family life for Kurt Vonnegut had come apart. The 1960s were a difficult decade for him, for professional reasons. The story market among the old family weeklies had dried up. Paperback originals could net a fair advance, but not garner serious reviews, and hence were not reputation-building. Switching to hardcover novels did not work for him, either—although there were some reviews, nothing until the decade's end sold well at all. With his children approaching college age, fill-in jobs were no longer enough, and so in 1965 he was forced to leave his family in Massachusetts and come by himself to the University of Iowa, where he taught creative writing for two years. That was a test of his marriage as well. But publisher Seymour Lawrence intervened with a three-book contract, a Guggenheim Fellowship got him out of Iowa City, and by 1968 Kurt was back in West Barnstable, writing *Slaughterhouse-Five*.

The success of that novel shows that however difficult the 1960s were for his profession, the cultural changes of that decade were not too much for his writing to handle. Much like "The Hyannis Port Story," his novels began working with the new cultural factors that accompanied and followed the Kennedy presidency. While the America of 1960 might not seem all that different from 1950, the country in 1970 was a world apart from both. With his works of the coming decade—*Mother Night; Cat's Cradle; God Bless You, Mr. Rosewater;* and, above all, *Slaughterhouse-Five* and the essays later collected as *Wampeters, Foma & Granfalloons*—Kurt Vonnegut articulated the terms of that transition with a structure that everyone could understand.

2

VONNEGUT'S
1960s

―――――――――――――――

Apocalypse Redone

In the 1950s, a period of relative stability in America culture, Kurt Vonnegut had faced challenges by shoring up older values. Not sociopolitical ones, as conservative thinkers would have them, but anthropological foundations such as the family structure and benefits of a folk society where everyone had purposeful work and a sense of value. The 1960s, of course, were anything but stable. "Family values" would become a politically loaded term, while patriotism, for some, would lose its civic quality and take on prowar shadings. Obviously an old fashioned *Collier's* or *Saturday Evening Post* story could not answer to these problems. But that was hardly the issue, as the magazines themselves would not survive, casualties of the same forces that threatened to undo the old order. Something new was needed.

Still tasked with supporting his family, the author adapted to the professional requirements of these new times. He diversified, using his ingenuity to land contracts for paperback originals, refining his art to follow editors from the paperback houses into hardcover publication, and devising material that would qualify as feature journalism for the more contemporary style of magazine, such as *Esquire* and *Harper's,* that could handle all this cultural change with comfort and even relish. In each of these undertakings, though, Vonnegut was less willing to promote cultural change than to question it. Indeed his interrogations anticipate the style subsequently established as postmodernism. Here previously unquestioned assumptions were submitted to rigorous examination, their supposedly natural underpinnings revealed to be utter fabrications. For more than half a century, anthropologists had been doing much the same, showing how cultures are human inventions, their realities being persuasive accounts but no more. Now writers and thinkers were doing it too. Some called these literary demolitions deconstruction. In Kurt Vonnegut's hands, they became this plus something more, a demonstration of how things can be not only built up and broken down, but ultimately refashioned in a useful way.

Mother Night (1961), *Cat's Cradle* (1963), *God Bless You, Mr. Rosewater* (1965), and *Slaughterhouse-Five* (1969) are the author's novels of this decade. Only the last received much attention—but so much that the others, plus *Player Piano* and *The Sirens of Titan* from the 1950s, were rushed back into print to satisfy readers' sudden hunger for anything by this newly popular writer. Some critics have argued that Kurt Vonnegut toiled in obscurity for twenty years because it took him that long to devise a way of writing about the destruction of Dresden, the ostensible subject of *Slaughterhouse-Five.* The truth is that America was not ready for a novel such as *Slaughterhouse-Five* any earlier than when it finally did appear. Not in the 1940s, the 1950s, or even most of the 1960s. The radical transitions of this last decade had to be accomplished and widely recognized before the story of Billy Pilgrim's experience—of Dresden and of so much more—could be appreciated. In other words the 1960s had to happen. One sees them happening, evolving slowly but steadily, in the author's work of that decade.

Mother Night, for example, is ostensibly about World War II as well. But, more important, it is about certain aspects of that war being remembered, remembered at the dawn of the 1960s, when so much would change. This is the era not of the Holocaust but of coming to terms with it—in some cases aggressively, as in the Israeli kidnaping of the Nazi killer Adolf Eichmann and putting him on trial for crimes against humanity. This was a highly publicized trial, the center of world attention as Vonnegut concocted his tale for a paperback originals market, where books could appear in a matter of weeks. Another novelist, Leon Uris, was responding to the same developments. Not just political developments, but cultural ones, such as Jews being presented not as victims but as fighters in novels such as *Exodus* and *Mila 18.* In his own remaking of perception, Vonnegut goes a step farther. After a quarter century of seeing Nazis as grotesque, horrifying, despicable monsters, he has them appear quite differently in *Mother Night:* as human beings, whose day at the office in the Ministry of Propaganda can just as easily involve an intramural Ping-Pong tournament as promoting mass murder. This is indeed risky, and in some quarters Kurt paid the price for it. Instead of solemnly intoning the well-known numbers of Nazi victims, he gives the tournament's scores. To make things worse, he has Adolf Eichmann offer the novel's narrator, a fellow prisoner also about to be tried for Holocaust crimes, a few hundred thousand of his own six million to spice up the memoir. Propaganda chief Dr. Joseph Goebbels is not portrayed as a madman; instead he's seen admiring the rhetoric of Lincoln's Gettysburg Address. Nor is Adolf Hitler shown as coldly soulless; Goebbels's reading of President Lincoln's speech brings him to sentimental tears. Meanwhile, across the Atlantic, President Franklin D. Roosevelt's favorite entertainment is this same Nazi ministry's abhorrent broadcasts, the ridiculousness of which makes him laugh with glee.

There's a logic to this, you see. Roosevelt is one of just three men (the others are American intelligence people) who know that the "best" of these broadcasts, being made by the novel's protagonist, American expatriate Howard W. Campbell, Jr., are in fact coded messages to the Allies regarding strategic moves by their enemy, for whom he's working as a classic double agent. The novel's more serious business concerns this role: can persons counterfeit an identity and survive morally intact? Is there a secret self, hidden inside, that is a good, decent person, while everything on the outside is just an insincere act? Campbell learns that you can't, that we are what we pretend to be, and had therefore better be very careful about what we pretend to be. In the end, he is on trial for crimes against humanity that he only technically didn't commit. He hangs himself before the judicial process begins, even though the day's mail has brought him a letter of exoneration from his old boss at U.S. Intelligence. What is Campbell's reason for suicide? That he's executing himself, not for crimes against humanity but for crimes against himself.

Mother Night ends with more than just the personal apocalypse of a single American agent. Campbell has been a writer; the success of his plays in Germany during the 1930s was what caused him to move there from America. The subject of those plays became the love-refuge he and his German wife had fashioned. But his role in the war destroyed that, too, as even his wife and in-laws accepted as truth, for inspiration, the most ridiculous of his coded broadcasts. The more unbelievable his satire was to him, the more of a truth it became to them, because they so dearly wanted to believe, even in an unsupportable, let alone lost, cause. And so love and art—specifically the love of art and the art of love—become casualties as well.

We are what we pretend to be. That's a perfect formulation of how a postmodernist views existence. The only things exceptional are how early Kurt Vonnegut came to this understanding and how effectively he was able to use it as the theme and structure of a novel. *Therefore we should be careful about what we pretend to be.* Right there is Vonnegut's special contribution to the postmodern understanding. True, in *Mother Night* the protagonist has not been careful and has paid the price. But this formulation also allows the possibility that, with care, a meaningful identity can be fabricated. Not discovered, but *made*. *Slaughterhouse-Five* would implement this.

Mother Night's remaking of the Nazi scene was potentially offensive enough to get its author prematurely identified as a black humorist. This term, having nothing to do with race but everything with a superficial tone of dark comedy, was used in the early 1960s to describe the otherwise troublesome manner of a wide variety of writers, from Terry Southern to Bruce Jay Friedman, who had nothing in common beyond an ability to shock. By the mid-1960s critics were better able to sort things out, based on the uses to which authors put this humor. Far beyond making sick jokes for simple shock value, Kurt Vonnegut was joshing a bit with the Nazis in order to make an important point. Indeed the Nazis were horrible—horrible *people*. If they are portrayed simply in terms of their crimes, crimes that often surpass the imagination's ability to truly comprehend, readers wind up with cartoon characters. Grotesque, hideous, abominable caricatures to be sure, but cartoon figures nonetheless—and therefore not necessary to be humanly comprehended. How can such propensity for evil ever be understood, if our rhetoric invites us to treat such atrocities as something not human at all?

This same determination to keep human beings responsible for comprehending the nature of evil they may do motivates the author's next novel, *Cat's Cradle*. For it he resurrects an institution first described (futuristically) in *Player Piano*, the research laboratory of General Forge and Foundry in Ilium, New York. Pointedly based on the author's experience writing publicity for General Electric in Schenectady-Albany-Troy, New York, the Ilium Works had in the earlier novel produced a fully automated world. For *Cat's Cradle* the setting is contemporary (1963), and like *Mother Night* this novel involves a contemporaneous understanding of an event two decades in the past. Here that event is a specific one from World War II, the detonation of the first atomic bomb over Hiroshima on August 6, 1945. This is "the day the world ended," a phrase the novel's protagonist hopes to use metaphorically as the title of his book about how the atomic bomb was developed and then used. But in an apocalypse immensely larger than Howard Campbell's in *Mother Night*, this new protagonist's writing manages to turn metaphor into reality. His investigation leads to the literal end of the world, as life on earth is frozen out of existence by means of a chemical formula an Ilium scientist has innocently devised.

Innocently devised? That's the joke of *Cat's Cradle*, and it shows the author's insight into how human beings can get themselves into so much trouble. Their brains, he suggests, are well in advance of their moral powers. Much later, in

Galápagos, Vonnegut takes advantage of one million years of projected history to let humanity devolve into a state of simple brute innocence. But here in *Cat's Cradle* the innocence is simply that of thoughtlessness, of a fascination with tinkering so strong that it can't even fathom a destructive consequence (think of how *Player Piano* ends).

In Vonnegut's novel the inventor of the atomic bomb is not a grotesque monster or even a warped genius driven by devilish ambition, two handy cartoon figures often used for such purpose. Instead he's an amiable if distracted father, who when he had a wife would absent-mindedly tip her when having breakfast before an important occasion. By the time of *Cat's Cradle's* action, he's widowed, but still has children at home. The eldest, Angela, is in charge, as little brother Newt recalls for the narrator when describing how his father created the first nuclear weapon. Pausing one day to wonder how turtles retract their heads, the man had proceeded to fill his lab with dozens of dime-store pets in aquariums, becoming so interested in them that all his atomic research came to a halt. When administrators from the Manhattan Project visit to find out what might be the problem, Angela treats it just like everything she's had to do since taking over her late mother's duties. Sending her father off to conduct atomic research was no different than packing off her brothers to school, and so getting him back on track demands nothing more exotic than having the administrators sneak into Dr. Hoenikker's lab and remove anything and everything involved with turtles. "He just came to work the next day and looked for things to play with and think about," we learn, "and everything there was to play with and think about had something to do with the bomb" (24).

So much for Dr. Felix Hoenikker's invention of catastrophic weaponry in World War II. At present, he's been asked by a general if something could be devised to solve any army's biggest problem, which is mud. *Ice-9,* a formulation that drastically raises the freezing temperature of water, does the job. No more mud! But once set loose, it freezes everything. So much for life on earth. Yet even that catastrophe is not staged futuristically, or even exotically. Instead, it is prompted by doings of the Hoenikker family—haplessly dysfunctional, by the way, as so many families in the 1960s were becoming, Vonnegut's included, as son Mark would recall in *The Eden Express.*

The single apparently exotic element in the novel is the religious leader Bokonon, who preaches a new style of theology on the poverty-stricken island of San Lorenzo in the Caribbean. Bokonon is a pseudonym. In truth the man is a castaway who washed up on the island forty years ago and who in response to his own and the island people's hopelessness devised a religion that would answer simple human need.

That religion, called Bokononism, is a refinement of Reverend Lasher's anthropological understanding of human usefulness from *Player Piano* and Winston Niles Rumfoord's Church of God the Utterly Indifferent in *The Sirens of Titan*. (For that matter, it also serves as an antidote to the "Nation of Two" Howard Campbell and his wife try to substitute for any larger belief in *Mother Night;* for a professed agnostic, Kurt Vonnegut does seem to have religion on his mind.) Its structure is simple, based on an artificial dualism that motivates people to strive for the one while struggling against the other. Quite plainly this is not just the structure of all religions but the essence of human understanding, the necessity and impossibility of reconciling the One with the Other. It's conventional religion, however, that capitalized the terms, that posits the One as an absolute reality, a principle informed by superior authority, an authority outside of human life—in other words, God. Bokononism will have none of that. Instead the religion's self-conscious sense of artifice remains paramount. This is why its members, the people of San Lorenzo, are so happy. "They were all employed full time as actors in a play they understood," the narrator learns, "that any human being anywhere could understand and applaud" (144). Here are the familiar elements of Vonnegut's canon, already established in his family-magazine stories and first four novels: a structure that gives people a sense of purpose and something to do, all without imposing a fraudulent sense of meaning (make that Meaning) that detracts from life itself.

Life does come to an end at the close of *Cat's Cradle:* by the agency of ice, not fire (alternatives suggested by the poet Robert Frost), but with neither a bang nor a whimper (the limits of modernist understanding as voiced by T. S. Eliot). Instead it all ends with a laugh. And not an empty, nihilistic one, either. Rather, in a way that would soon typify the postmodern attitude, Vonnegut expresses the putative end of existence not just as having been a practical joke, but by playing that joke out to its logical consequence. There's certainly an energy to the universe, but arguing whether it's benevolent or malevolent is a waste of time, not to mention a self-destructive obsession. Instead the energy of the joke is sustained, rebounded back to its source. If existence has been merely a game, here at least the ball is kept in play. How much better this is than sobbing in the disappointment of loss or arguing with the referee. *Cat's Cradle* ends like those Laurel and Hardy movies that the author cherished and that sustained him and the rest of America during the Great Depression. Life fails, in a heartbreakingly yet adorably loveable manner. There's no hope, of course, but we sympathize with the effort—and are amused.

There's plenty of amusement in Vonnegut's next novel, *God Bless You, Mr. Rosewater*, but it's of a painful, sometimes even mean variety. Perhaps that's so because there's no religion in the novel—other than the deity mentioned in the title. The meanness is understandable, as the attitude is directed toward money, something of which the author had precious little in 1964. That's the year he was forced to begin writing personal journalism for the more sophisticated magazines that had survived the television-induced advertising blight. (Eventually he'd prosper in journalism, but only with convincing that such work deserved to be saved, as it would be in *Wampeters, Foma & Granfalloons;* Kurt's revenge on us for arguing for this work was to title it with nonsensical terms from Bokononism.)

There had been rough economic patches before, when sales of short stories to the family magazines had been slow. But in the 1950s he'd always managed to support his family with fill-in jobs. Some were amusing, as the day in 1954 he spent at *Sports Illustrated,* a new magazine that was under the gun to dress up its writing. So it hired some novelists, Kurt Vonnegut included. His first assignment was to report on how a racehorse at Aqueduct had shied at the starter's pistol and leaped over the infield railing. How does one dress up that? After an hour's thought, he typed a single line onto the sheet of paper and walked out. The line read, "The horse jumped over the fucking fence." Years later, seeking a spot of brightness in their obituary tributes to the man, other writers would recall this incident with bemusement and sympathy. Trying to sell the first Saab automobiles in America was funny enough to produce an after-dinner entertainment subsequently included in the introduction to *Bagombo Snuff Box.* Some work was interesting, such as writing promotional copy for a foundry in Boston whose industrial castings were not only state of the art but works of art in themselves. Other work was conscientious and inspiring, such as teaching in a school for emotionally disturbed students ("problem children," as they were called in the 1950s) near home in Cape Cod.

There had even been genuine traumas to face, such as when the death of Kurt's father in 1957 put him in a yearlong writer's block. He came out of it only to face an even grimmer practical joke, the death of his sister and brother-in-law and the need to adopt their children, even though economic straits would make this a trying time indeed.

But, by the time of writing *God Bless You, Mr. Rosewater,* Kurt Vonnegut's luck at improvising an income seemed to have run out. Book reviews for *Life,* travel essays for *Venture,* even a *New York Times* review of *The Random House Dictionary* (you think the horse jumping over the fence was a challenge?)—in circumstances such as these, a small advance to write a novel, one no more likely to sell any better than his first four had, was hardly cause for celebration. Rather it was a reminder of just how bad his economic times were.

"A sum of money is a leading character in this tale about people," *God Bless You, Mr. Rosewater* begins, "just as a sum of honey might properly be a leading character in a tale about bees" (15). Here are not only the parameters of Kurt Vonnegut's fifth novel, but a demonstration of its logic; just about everything that happens in the book devolves from this stated first principle.

First principles, we should know by now, were alien to this writer's fiction. In none of his previous works did he introduce ruling absolutes, and, where others would have them, he'd promptly undertake a deconstruction of their presumed necessity. What Kurt Vonnegut believed in evolved from present circumstances, such as groups of human beings either forming themselves into happy folk societies or, unhappily, not. His religions (or substitutes for religions) were self-apparently artificial, their artifice being much of the fun. Therefore it is an important sign—quite possibly a bad one—that the author starts out this new book with such an absolutistic line.

The interest in *God Bless You, Mr. Rosewater,* then, is how the narrative deals with this problem. Does it work its way out of the box or succumb to it? The sum of money does, like a real character, have a life of its own: the capital amount is not only huge, approaching 100 million dollars (in 1965 dollars—quadruple that now) but by virtue of compound interest is growing by a remarkable amount each year, and by a significant measure each day. Other characters, more properly human, exert contrary forces on this money, not so much fighting over it for themselves as working to define its nature—remember the postmodernist understanding of how reality is a description. Were this a conventional narrative, the author could turn to the device that would accomplish half the work automatically: having one rival character be bad, while the other is good. The side that would manipulate money for unfair personal gain is certainly bad, and by the novel's third page Vonnegut has made its agent appear not only despicable but embarrassingly awkward, an object of not just moral scorn but of high schoolish ridicule, simply because as a lawyer he has sniffed out the possibility that a large amount of cash may be changing hands in the Rosewater family.

This was the era, after all, in which torts and litigation had become so common that lawyer jokes abounded. A client asks an attorney, "How much do you charge?," and is told, "One thousand dollars to answer three questions." "Isn't that a lot of money?," the client stammers. "Yes, it is," the lawyer responds, adding, "and what's your third question?" Vonnegut maintains this cynical mood by starting off attorney Norman Mushari's resume with typical facts but adding his ancestry (son of a Brooklyn rug merchant), height (five foot three), and this physical characteristic: that "He had an enormous ass, which was luminous when bare" (17). Hired because the firm's partners need "a touch more viciousness" in their operations, Mushari fills the bill. But repulsive as his nature is, it fails to tip the balance in favor of his opponent, Eliot Rosewater, the socially conscious president of the Rosewater Foundation who would use these multimillions for simple human good. Introduced as a progressive thinker (by manner of a heartfelt if bitterly expressed letter meant to be read by his eventual successor, but filched by Mushari as evidence of the man's madness), Rosewater turns out to be no Eugene V. Debs (one of Kurt Vonnegut's personal heroes), nor even a practical reformer adept at getting aid to those who need it most. Instead Eliot is a slovenly drunk who can be as thoughtlessly cruel as he is sincerely humanitarian. His plan for doing good amounts to little more than handing out ten-dollar bills to persons who are about that amount short. Simply to keep up with the capital sum's earnings, he'd have to disperse ten thousand dollars per day—every day, Vonnegut notes, Sundays included. If the existence of all that money is a temptation to evil, Eliot's attempted depletion of it seems hopeless indeed.

Perhaps life itself has become hopeless for this character, demoralized since an incident in World War II, when, as a combat infantryman, he shot and killed a presumedly dangerous enemy soldier who turned out to be a young boy. As if seeking absolution, not just for his sin but for the sins of the world, Eliot makes gestures at being Christlike, counseling any successor at the foundation to "Be generous. Be kind. You can safely ignore the arts and sciences. They never helped anybody. Be a sincere, attentive friend of the poor" (23).

To do just that, Eliot moves out of the fancy Rosewater Foundation offices in New York City and relocates in Rosewater, Indiana, the family's original home and source of wealth, generated by Civil War armaments profiteering. In a walk-up office over a lunchroom and liquor store, he starts trying to save the world—not just one person at a time, but one minor, inconsequential problem at a time. Elsewhere Kurt Vonnegut talks about the Indiana of his own childhood as an Elysium; here it is portrayed as a land so deathly flat, with a people so deathly dull, that Eliot's haplessness fits right in. Such is the power of money, or rather the powerlessness of not having it. Not that the rich, or even those doing just OK in the middle class, seem much better, as their thoughtless self-absorption prompts the poorer souls around them to wonder who on earth can have the intelligence to be running things.

The great majority of God Bless You, Mr. Rosewater's narrative is devoted to this world, a world equally bleak whether rich or poor. Poverty is a trap, but

wealth is no way out of it—no happily redeeming way, at least. But readers
haven't yet lost faith in the author working his way out of this economic box,
and at the novel's very end a solution is found. The character who provides it
is Kilgore Trout, a science-fiction writer Kurt Vonnegut would use, off and on,
in other novels all the way to his last, *Timequake* (1997). He appears in *God
Bless You. Mr. Rosewater* to make good on Eliot's challenge, early in the narrative, to a convention of science-fiction writers he tasks with something truly
fantastic, which is to acknowledge the hugely transformative power of money,
to "think about the silly ways money gets passed around now," and—most
important—"then think up better ways" (31).

When Kilgore Trout shows up at the novel's end with an answer, one might
call him a deus ex machina, a god from a machine hoisted into the action to
resolve matters that would otherwise remain impossible. But Trout is no god.
For the next three decades Kurt Vonnegut would call him many things, including, most accurately, an aged and frightened Jesus whose sentence to crucifixion had been commuted to one of life imprisonment. Perhaps this is how the
well-intentioned Vonnegut saw himself. He did state in interviews, time and
again, that Trout was an image of what he himself might have become, an awkwardly comic, pathetically overlooked science-fiction writer. At the time of
God Bless You, Mr. Rosewater, Vonnegut was the closest he'd ever be to this, yet
he sustains a noble role for Trout, which is to reinvent the terms of existence.

Others had tried in earlier novels. Howard Campbell, for example, had
only pretended to be evil, while hiding his essential good inside. This was
wrong, the author said. "We are what we pretend to be," Vonnegut wrote in
Mother Night's introduction, "so we must be careful about what we pretend to
be" (v). Now, in *God Bless You, Mr. Rosewater,* he puts the second half of that
statement into action. In the first of his five novels, which is utterly bereft of
religion, this statement is allowed to stand, a motto on the wall in the welcoming shelter of a mental hospital: "Pretend to be good always, and even God will
be fooled" (203). This notion begins the book's last chapter, the chapter in
which Kilgore Trout, although cited before, will now appear to take command
of the resolution.

Appropriately for a novel written by an author at crucial junctures in both
his life and career, it was a major step forward. Kurt Vonnegut's earlier works
had demonstrated how personal meaningfulness is created by having a sense of
being useful, of being needed. But for the economic climate of *God Bless You,
Mr. Rosewater,* there is a serious problem, one that it takes Kilgore Trout to
identify: "How to love people who have no use?" (210).

Can anyone do this? Kilgore Trout offers evidence of at least one group of people who do, volunteer firefighters: "They rush to the rescue of any human being, and count not the cost. The most contemptible man in town, should his contemptible house catch fire, will see his enemies put the fire out. And, as he pokes through the ashes for remains of his possessions, he will be comforted and pitied by no less than the Fire Chief" (211).

From this example of people treasuring people, we must learn, Trout urges. As a science-fiction writer, he offers more such examples, here and in subsequent Vonnegut narratives, which are fantastic to be sure, but are hopefully implementable as new, more persuasive descriptions of reality. *Any* other description of reality would be better than the one currently passing as credible in the world of *God Bless You, Mr. Rosewater.* In the work of writers like Trout, there may be real hope. And Kurt Vonnegut himself is the best example of a writer whose fiction has genuinely done some good. Trout's appearance has been announced by the motto that if one pretends to be good, even God will be fooled. A better role for pretense cannot be imagined.

What about that troublesome sum of money, the root of so much trouble? At the novel's start, Eliot had been seen advising whoever, as heir, would succeed him as president of the Rosewater Foundation. Now, inspired by Trout, he changes not the role of the foundation but the nature of who will be his heir. Henceforth it will be every child ever born in Rosewater County, with every one of them entitled to a share of the Rosewater wealth. Like *Cat's Cradle,* this novel ends with a laugh, and the last laugh is Eliot's, at the expense of the connivers who had schemed to skim off this money for themselves. As a new description of reality, the Rosewater inheritance is now safely dispersed.

The description of reality Kurt Vonnegut himself was living began changing within months of this fifth novel's publication. Most immediately, it became his first to be seriously reviewed and also the first to go into a second printing. Nothing big, just a second run of seven thousand copies to complement the first six thousand (less a stimulant of sales than the publisher's belief that reviews in big-city newspapers and national magazines would prompt bookstore orders). The advance, however, had been received and spent a year before that, and, even with another several thousand copies available for purchase, such royalties could never support a family, especially a family of eight with kids getting ready for college. And so the author took the first substantial job he'd had since working for General Electric, which was heading off to college himself—signing on to teach creative writing at the University of Iowa. The move was not an easy one, as his wife and children stayed behind. It was lonesome; in his second year, daughter Edie, finishing high school, joined him as company.

The importance of Iowa City has many dimensions. It did take Kurt away from his wife and family, but it gave him something of compensatory delight: an extended family in the community of writers and students that, more than being just a college, made existence here a distinct way of life. Extended families, folk societies, organizations for the fun of it—all his life Kurt Vonnegut had loved such things. Wherever he went in life, be it the new world of public schools, both high school and college, military service, or publicity work at GE, he would relish the basis for social membership. The more improvised it was, the better. And nothing was unacceptable because of intellectual style. A college fraternity and an infantry platoon were great ways of having "brothers" and "buddies," however artificial the format. *The more artificial, the better,* Vonnegut would say, in harmony with his novels and short stories, because here is the demonstration that humankind, by virtue of imaginative creativity, can make something better of its circumstances.

College teaching was something boldly new for him, of course. And quite challenging, for he'd left Cornell without a bachelor's degree and Chicago without his master's. The only piece of paper he had was a high school diploma, a fact that placed him at the absolute bottom of the University of Iowa's salary scale. It became cruelly ironic that in 1971 a new dean at Chicago noticed this lack and ordered an earned degree to be awarded, with the novel *Cat's Cradle* serving as master's thesis; while teaching at Iowa, Kurt had tried repeatedly to have the Anthropology Department accept the thesis he'd submitted in 1947, simply to get a much needed raise, but without success. By 1971 the dean was responding not to need but to the embarrassment of Vonnegut's having become a great success despite the University of Chicago's lack of academic endorsement. Kurt wasn't bitter; he accepted the degree with courtesy and bought himself a class of 1971 letter sweater, wearing it with pride for photographs accompanying the news story.

Yet the challenge remained in 1965: what was he going to teach these students?

"Don't tell them everything you know in the first hour," a sympathetic colleague counseled him.

"That wasn't the problem," Kurt recalls. "I was able to tell them everything I knew in the first two minutes."

In truth he was a gifted teacher, eventually having to give it up because it consumed so much of his time. Admittedly he wasn't a famous writer just then, but he was a veteran of "nearly sixty sales to the slicks," as a moderator introduced him to a workshop session. *He'd worked as a professional,* and becoming a pro was the ideal of every student in attendance. And what a thoughtful, conscientious, and dedicated new teacher they had. What Kurt joked about—the fact that he'd just realized that he was forty-three years old and had never read *Madame Bovary,* for example—actually stimulated him to catch up on such classics. So he read Flaubert and also newer authors such as Theodore Roethke and Louis-Ferdinand Céline. His students benefitted, but so did his work; Roethke and Céline play prominent roles in bringing *Slaughterhouse-Five* into being, so credited in the novel's first chapter.

But there is a more important factor in Kurt Vonnegut's life, a factor directly linked to his style of writing, that helps explain the transition he underwent in the mid-1960s. It too was economically motivated, because the same circumstances that had forced him to take a full-time job in Iowa City had prompted him to try new markets with new literary forms, given that the old markets and old forms were no longer there for him. Late in 1964, with the advance from *God Bless You, Mr. Rosewater* running out, the author took on a journalistic assignment, writing a personal essay about his family's hometown, West Barnstable, Massachusetts. Good enough to be collected and stand with what he considered the best of his short stories in *Welcome to the Monkey House,* the Barnstable piece earned its status by being what critics were just beginning to call the New Journalism, a highly individual style of writing in which the writer used all the techniques of fiction, including characterization, imagery, symbolism, and development by dialogue, in order to convey a deeper, truer sense of the reality at hand. Dan Wakefield had done this in *Island in the City* (1959). Joan Didion, Tom Wolfe, and most spectacularly Hunter S. Thompson followed. Of all these writers, Vonnegut employed a new method that shared the most with Thompson's, for, in addition to the tools of fiction both writers used their own reactions as an important substance of the story. This was personal journalism in spades.

The next year Vonnegut did five reviews for *Life* and the *New York Times Book Review,* and in 1966 there were another five, including the *Random House Dictionary* review that brought him to Seymour Lawrence's attention. This and the others were written in an extremely personal manner. To make sense of the otherwise exotic plot in Friedrich Dürrenmatt's new novel, Kurt compared it to the petty doings of office politics back in the publicity bureau of GE; the educational insights of Bel Kaufman's *Up the Down Staircase* made sense to him only when recalled in terms of his own (and every reader's) high school years. Readers loved it. Editors asked for more, including another travel piece and an essay on the unfairness of being labeled a science-fiction writer. Kurt Vonnegut could explain, in commonly understandable yet inventively funny ways, just why cruising on the Kennedy yacht was more commonplace than one might imagine (he did it only because the skipper was a Cape Cod neighbor and the boat was being moved). And also why science-fiction fans overdid their enthusiasms, to the detriment of writers with larger aspirations. "They are particularly hot for Kafka," he noted for the *New York Times Book Review,* as collected in *Wampeters, Foma & Granfalloons.* "Boomers of science fiction," he complained, try to include within their favorite subgenre not just George Orwell but Ralph Ellison and Gustave Flaubert as well. "They often say things like that," Vonnegut added. "Some are crazy enough to try to capture Tolstoy. It is as though I were to claim that everybody of note belonged fundamentally to Delta Upsilon, my own lodge, incidentally, whether he knew it or not. Kafka would have made a desperately unhappy D.U." (4).

Between 1964, when the author was at the bottom of his worst earnings cycle, and 1970, when the success of *Slaughterhouse-Five* had made him not only a well-paid writer but an international celebrity, Kurt Vonnegut published thirty-four pieces of short nonfiction. What he considered the best of them, plus a few more selected from the continuing stream, were collected in 1974 as *Wampeters, Foma & Granfalloons.* This volume is important for several reasons. Analytically it shows Vonnegut undertaking the major development in his writing that would bring him both literary success and great public fame. That, quite simply, consisted in the incorporation of himself as an integral part of his writing—making himself present as its author and furthermore making that act of authorship a key part of the narrative itself. Historically this development parallels a heating up of the American 1960s themselves. In this latter case the writing may not have changed (from its personalized method of 1964), but the country certainly did. By the decade's end America was ready for the way Kurt Vonnegut wrote, just as he himself was now prepared to present himself to these challenging new times.

The range of his personal journalism spans topics from popular culture to world politics—from the Transcendental Meditation craze, for example, to the tragedy of mass starvation in Biafra. His essay on the Maharishi Mahesh Yogi is titled "Yes, We Have No Nirvanas"; appearing in the June 1968 issue of *Esquire,* it engages the topic as popular culture and is whimsical in nature. "Biafra: A People Betrayed," published in June 1970 in *McCall's,* handles more serious business—immensely more serious, for the breakaway nation was undergoing a programmatic genocide imposed by rival Nigeria. Kurt Vonnegut did the first piece when he was still unknown, the second after he'd become famous. Yet for all the differences between the two subjects and his own status when addressing them, the author uses the same basic structure to produce an essay: not just employing the techniques of fiction, but applying them in a way that makes his own involvement the center of attention.

Is this a fraudulent method, or perhaps even a selfish one? Not at all. By the end of the 1960s, both the Maharishi and Biafra had been covered exhaustively. Indeed they were such dominant elements in popular and political consciousness that not only was it hard to have a fresh thought about them, it was easy to handle them with attitudes gone rigid from overuse. The last thing needed at the time was a blue-ribbon commission report on either, as too many such reports had virtually fossilized our response. We all knew about the Maharishi and his style of Transcendental Meditation, and we all knew about the suffering in Biafra. Or did we? Vonnegut's new method showed us what we did not know, because we'd never experienced either personally. Through the agency of his essays, we now could.

Kurt's Maharishi piece begins with an admitted conflict of interest: his wife and eighteen-year-old daughter are hooked on Transcendental Meditation. Were this a conventional essay, the author would have followed tradition and recused himself from the assignment; journalists, like judges, are supposed to be unprejudiced. At the very least, a traditional author would have taken his disclaimer seriously, making sure to keep his story unaffected. But instead Vonnegut does the opposite, bringing up his family's involvement at key points and always in familiar, vernacular terms of complaint. Does meditation work? Well, his wife and daughter are serene. "Nothing pisses them off anymore," he notes, adding that "They glow like bass drums with lights inside" (32). Is the Maharishi capitalizing on such facile joy, making millions? Well, he charges fifty dollars per person, discounted to thirty-five dollars for students and housewives. What does this mean for the writer? "I've got seventy goddamn simoleons in this new religion so far" (32).

By calling it a religion, Vonnegut generates the conflict that becomes his essay's theme: adherents to TM insist it is *not* a religion, but rather a technique. As such it strikes the author as too easy, demanding none of the rigors of belief, or even the artifice of belief, like his own fictive faiths. The rapture these adherents describe strikes him as frivolous, no better than the effects of drugs and alcohol, for which he uses the commonest slang terms.

What this use of the vernacular does is bring an exotic Eastern practice down to the level of a trite Western one, which in its triteness can then be dismissed. Vonnegut does not claim the practitioners are being victimized. No, he himself is the victim, out seventy dollars and sore about it, and also angry with himself that he's wasted his time, listening to all this prattle about easiness and self-help: "I went outside the hotel after that, liking Jesus better than I ever liked Him before. I wanted to see a crucifix, so I could say to it, 'You know why You're up there? It's Your own fault. You should have practiced Transcendental Meditation, which is easy as pie. You would also have been a better carpenter'" (39–40).

For his Biafra essay, Kurt Vonnegut does much the same, not reporting on his subject but rather embracing it so thoroughly that he can articulate it simply by expressing himself, the more familiar and commonly accessible the better. Who had been to a session with the Maharishi? Not all that many of *Esquire's* readers, to be sure. But virtually every one of them knew the ire at being bilked out of seventy dollars. Who'd been to Biafra during its terrible civil war with Nigeria? Just a few Americans at most. But the author had been one of them. And what he felt there he most sincerely wanted his readers to feel, for only this way can future tragedies of this sort be avoided.

Early on in the piece, Vonnegut notes some comic touches among the Biafran leaders and gets scolded for it. "You won't open your mouth unless you can make a joke," the American woman who's hosting his visit complains. "It was true," Kurt confesses, but makes an important distinction: "Joking was my response to misery I couldn't do anything about" (146).

This dilemma shapes his essay. Just as his disgust with the hullabaloo over Transcendental Meditation led him through that piece, touching on this or that aspect of the Maharishi's technique with examples of how they were quite pettily affecting the writer, "Biafra: A People Betrayed" wrestles with the author's inability to improve matters. Africa, after all, is so far from home to Americans that many have trouble getting a clear picture of it, much less being able to help (beyond the abstraction of charitable donations). In his trip two decades later to Mozambique, where another war was causing more suffering, Vonnegut expressed this attitude more bitterly. For the readers of *Parade* magazine, the Sunday newspaper supplement, published on January 7, 1990, and for those looking into his 1991 collection *Fates Worse Than Death*, he presents an intimate picture of just how the suffering happens, but he frames the piece with a snapshot of himself among the people, described as such: "The photograph at the head of this chapter shows me in action in Mozambique, demonstrating muscular Christianity in an outfit that might have been designed by Ralph Lauren. The aborigines didn't know whether to shit or go blind until I showed up. And then I fixed everything" (175). Is Vonnegut making a cruel joke? Of course he is, but it's regarding misery he can't do anything about. And the fact that he can't do anything about it makes *him* the joke's target.

"Biafra: A People Betrayed" shows Kurt Vonnegut meeting Biafrans and learning many things about them—so many things, little and big, personal and profound, that his readers feel they know them, too. How their travail in being driven to the jungles was worsened by the fact that they are villagers, not jungle dwellers. How the fracture of their country was especially painful because of their kinship structure, whereby an extended family can number in the several hundreds. How their better educations got them the best jobs when Britain cobbled together an independent nation from two former colonies—and how their rivals hated them for that. How their national anthem consisted of the melody of *Finlandia* played on an ancient marimba.

Is the author's method logical? Not strictly, as it skips from one point of fascination to another. But one of those points involves the illogic of this whole tragedy. "It's hard to prove genocide," he's told. "If some Biafrans survive, then genocide hasn't been committed. If no Biafrans survive, who will complain?" (150). Vonnegut's essay ends with some tears, but more ably with a quick recall of his most striking memories of the trip, memories of a nation that no longer exists.

At the same time Kurt Vonnegut began writing his highly personalized style of New Journalism, his fiction underwent a transition in similar terms. As topics in the daily world were made more accessible by being reshaped in a fictive manner, so now the fiction he produced featured more and more persons, places, and things from actuality. President John F. Kennedy's function in "The Hyannis Port Story" had been more in terms of image than reality, but the man himself, distinctive voice and all, indeed made a personal appearance to end the story—and to make its most important point, about how the relationship with the Rumfoords was a neighborly matter after all. In *Slaughterhouse-Five*, however, Robert Kennedy, at the time a candidate in California's Democratic presidential primary, makes a real-life appearance, in sadly real time: on the occasion of his death, reported on the news as Kurt Vonnegut was finishing the last chapter of his novel. And the stuff of that novel is real, as well: not the satirized conflict of *Mother Night* but the actual Second World War, not fought by romanticized characters (as in so much conventional fiction) but by teenaged boys so innocent they might as well still be children. And among those boys is Kurt Vonnegut himself, not just identified as a character in the narrative three times but actively present in the novel's first and last chapters, in the very act of writing this book that readers were never asked to believe was about anything but itself.

Orienting his fiction to himself began in 1966, when, for the hardcover reissue of *Mother Night*, Kurt Vonnegut added an autobiographical introduction, explaining his personal experience with the "Nazi monkey business" this book characterized. For the first time in his writing career, he described the fire-bombing of Dresden—described it as he experienced it himself—even though the event wasn't included in the main text of *Mother Night*. Nor would it be in *Slaughterhouse-Five*—just the run-up to it and its aftereffects. But getting his experiences down on paper, creating the personal context for both novels, was important. From then on nearly every work of fiction Vonnegut published would feature just this kind of personal orientation. In *Slaughterhouse-Five* it would lead to his first great success and prove to be a technique that would see him through for another twenty-eight years, climaxing with the exceedingly personal nature of his last novel, *Timequake*, in which the narrative achieves a life of its own.

"All this happened, more or less," *Slaughterhouse-Five* begins, its narrative voice being the actual voice of its living author. By the time the novel ends, readers see that same author sitting at his typewriter in his Cape Cod home, finishing the book two nights after Robert Kennedy has been shot. That was not only something that had happened in history, but was an event still fresh in memory, especially as readers were likely to remember where they themselves were when hearing of both Kennedy brothers' deaths. Thus the reading of *Slaughterhouse-Five* becomes just as personal an undertaking as the writing of it and just as self-apparently a human act. The book is only apparently diverse. It is in fact an association of structures, from the autobiographical and historical to the fictive, a seeming aggregate over which hovers a sense of pri-mal power in singleness of purpose—a purpose directed to comprehending the work's own creation at the hand of writer and reader alike. Thus this structure is not a group, but a single mass, spontaneously subdividing into subsidiary forms as the narrative flows into various phases, each seeking expression in the appropriate form. Each of these forms, then, bears evidence of a controlling sense of story. And what a story it is! It is this coming to grips with the larger reality of the book's existence that infiltrates the mind of the observer, creating the feeling that what is at hand is a truly living thing.

Some of that infiltration happens subliminally. Can readers, especially first-time readers of the novel, be expected to note consciously that just as a very young Billy Pilgrim sees the radium face of his father's wristwatch glowing in the dark of Mammoth Cave, a somewhat older Billy, old enough to be a sol-dier but still quite childlike in his innocence, is led into a prisoner-of-war camp past lines of captured Russians, sick and malnourished, whose faces glow like radium watch dials? Or that the distinctive stripes on the prison train that brought him there match the colors of stripes on the caterer's tent serving his and his wife's wedding anniversary party? Or that four German guards are struck speechless by the spectacle of Dresden destroyed, as they stand there with their mouths open in silent harmony like a barbershop quartet, and that an amateur barbershop quartet will be part of the entertainment for that same party? These are but three correlations of many that pepper the novel, which itself jumps from scene to scene, from year to year, in no apparent order. Yet readers suspect there is an order to things, part of which has been accomplished by this subliminal linkage.

Consider what must be held together: the author sitting there at his type-writer, readers with the finished book in hand, and protagonist Billy Pilgrim hopscotching all over the times and spaces of his life. Indeed, "Billy Pilgrim has come unstuck in time" (20), his narrative begins, and although Vonnegut is able to give a chronological outline of his life in the next three pages (a helpful orientation for the reader, to be sure), for the next eight chapters almost every successive paragraph will have him in a different time and space, in no logical order. But that's the key to this structure, as the readers have been told up front: "Billy is spastic in time, has no control over where he is going next, and the trips aren't necessarily fun. He is in a constant state of stage fright, he says, because he never knows what part of his life he is going to have to act in next" (20).

Acting is the key element in living, *improvisatory* acting because one never knows where in life one is—to anyone familiar with the Vonnegut canon to date, and that would include many of this best seller's readers who created a market for paperback reprints and even hardcover reissues of the author's previous works, the circumstance Billy Pilgrim finds himself in at novel's start sounds familiar. We are what we pretend to be, so we'd better be careful who we pretend to be. Pretend to be good, and even God will be fooled. You think life must have a purpose? So then go invent one. These sentiments, from *Mother Night, God Bless You, Mr. Rosewater,* and *Cat's Cradle,* respectively, indicate how Billy's time travel is more than just a science-fiction device.

Were it imposed from the outside, by a science-fiction writer with a technical agenda, time travel could easily be just that. But it isn't imposed. Instead the notion arises from Billy's own circumstance, triggered by the understandable physical and emotional trauma of being the sole survivor of a plane crash, and even more so from the deeper wound he suffered in the war. Consider this scene from the war's aftermath, when the young man has been committed to a mental hospital for a time. For a roommate he gets Eliot Rosewater, in treatment for alcoholism, who introduces him to science fiction, in particular the works of Kilgore Trout:

Kilgore Trout became Billy's favorite living author, and science fiction became the only sort of tales he could read.

Rosewater was twice as smart as Billy, but he and Billy were dealing with similar crises in similar ways. They had both found life meaningless, partly because of what they had seen in war. Rosewater, for instance, had shot a fourteen-year-old fireman, mistaking him for a German soldier. So it goes. And Billy had seen the greatest massacre in European history, which was the firebombing of Dresden. So it goes.

So they were trying to re-invent themselves and their universe. Science fiction was a big help. (87)

Note the emphasis: meaning not discovered but *invented*. That's why science fiction, as a form of imaginative literature that foregrounds the reshaping of actuality, proves useful—not as a technical device, but as a metaphor for what is really happening in Billy's mind.

He's not crazy, but he does have an opinion, and, rather than writing science fiction itself (Kilgore Trout's job), he acts like a normal American and uses the commonly available venue for people, which is writing letters to the editor. Local papers welcome them and rarely consider their authors crackpots. Billy's belief that he has been abducted by outer-space aliens would indeed be considered insane except for one thing: he's using the experience not as an adventure tale but as an explanation for the nature of life. An explanation, an interpretation, an opinion, a metaphor—as the makings of a fiction, in other words. And creating fiction is the way we make sense of life. The act is improvisatory and self-consciously artificial, but that's how people make sense of an otherwise senseless condition. Any account of life is a description, and descriptions have their own reality. This has been the essence of Kurt Vonnegut's belief since his first stories and first novel, products of the early 1950s. Not until the end of the 1960s, however, was mainstream America ready to embrace it with such enthusiasm.

Remembering that *Slaughterhouse-Five* is principally a book about itself, about itself being written and itself being read, the role these outer-space aliens play is important. Tralfamadorians are not invaders. They are here only because they're curious about Earthlings, and for this reason: in the entire universe they've found only one place where inhabitants believe in free will, and that's Earth. Is such belief a bad thing? Only when it makes people feel responsible for everything that happens, which happens to be their natural proclivity. But doing so dodges a greater responsibility, which is to invent meaning as needed, improvised according to conditions at hand. Billy Pilgrim accepts this responsibility, which generates Kurt Vonnegut's own larger narrative.

When Vonnegut published *Slaughterhouse-Five,* its readers and reviewers made the predictable assumption that because both he and his fictive character were Dresden survivors, Billy Pilgrim's story was his own. In fact Vonnegut takes pains to identify himself in descriptions of the business in Germany as someone else, saying or doing something apart from Billy, as another person in the scene. And of course the author is physically present in chapters 1 and 10, writing the novel itself. It is this latter role that links him most closely with Billy, for our first glimpse of Billy Pilgrim is when he's at his typewriter, drafting another letter to the newspaper editor about his experiences—experiences not in Dresden, but on Tralfamadore. More than anything else, both he and Kurt are writers, present to the readers not as representations of some other story but as writers of the story at hand. Neither represents reality. Both of them invent it, because that's how meaning is formed. And Tralfamadore is just an image for that.

Even in terms of narrative action, the Tralfamadorians rise well above being simple science-fiction devices. What they've brought to Earth is not futuristic technology but rather a new understanding of time. That understanding relates to human purpose and meaning—that while the notion of free-will responsibility for the state of existence is ridiculous, people do have the power to devise their own descriptions of what matters in their worlds. This Tralfamadorian understanding is presented not in terms of science, or even of philosophy, but rather in literature (the most devalued concept of all in traditional science fiction). Tralfamadorian novels, just like Tralfamadorian life, have an entirely different nature from the chronological format common on Earth. To Billy these alien novels look like telegrams, with brief clumps of symbols divided by stars. His Tralfamadorian host corrects this view, advising that there are no telegrams as such on Tralfamadore. Even telegrams imply sequence, if only internally, and sequentiality is precisely what a Tralfamadorian novel avoids.

What do these outer-space novels embrace? For a Tralfamadorian, the answer is simple. Each clump of symbols "is a brief, urgent message," describing an important situation or scene. What makes them different is that they are read all at once, with simultaneity replacing sequence. Relationship among these parts isn't the point; totality is. "Their author has chosen them carefully," Billy learns, "so that, when seen all at once, they produce an image of life that is beautiful and surprising and deep." There are no beginnings or endings, just "the depth of many marvelous moments seen all at one time" (76).

Putting this description of innovative literary form in the midst of his own innovative novel is, for Vonnegut as for many writers of this age, no idle manner. Donald Barthelme had included a readers' questionnaire halfway through his novel *Snow White* (1967), asking how they liked the story, its characters, and its development so far. Steve Katz went even further, shaping *The Exagggerations [sic] of Peter Prince* (1968) as a continuous interaction among writer, reader, and the printed page. Doing this, they intended, would draw attention away from any suspension of disbelief and reinforce the novel's sense of artifice. Vonnegut's way of doing this had been to start and finish with accounts of his starting and finishing the book. Yet the narrative framed by this self-consciousness was wildly nontraditional on its own terms. And so it made sense to include a brief discussion of the literary theory explaining just how this new method worked.

How do we know Kurt Vonnegut wants such concerns about literary theory to be part of his work? Because late in the novel he has Billy Pilgrim take part in a broadcast devoted to the hottest critical topic of the day, the one that had motivated Barthelme, Katz, and a host of other innovationists: the presumed "death of the novel" and antidotes to it. Ronald Sukenick, whose novel *Up* (1968) is an exuberant display of narrative self-consciousness and reflexiveness, went so far as to title his collection of short fiction *The Death of the Novel and Other Stories* (1969). It is in this area, innovative fiction as opposed to science fiction, that Vonnegut finds the method for his own art. As for science fiction, that's something Billy finds not in seminars on the art but in pornographic bookstores, where Kilgore Trout's books serve as window dressing. Both science fiction and pornography, the author has said, offer false promises of hopelessly hospitable worlds.

As for Trout's novels and stories themselves, many of which are summarized in the course of *Slaughterhouse-Five,* they seem boldly exotic. They do serve Vonnegut's purpose well, because a great many works he may have wished to write (or perhaps didn't have the nerve or poor taste to write) can be cited as if they really existed, a technique another innovator, Jorge Luis Borges, celebrated as the "imaginary library." More important, it allows him to distance himself and his own narrative from the more extreme hypotheses Trout suggests. Some are indeed quite silly, part of his characterization as a bizarre eccentric. But Vonnegut has a way of signaling which of Trout's fictions he believes in, by creating parallel examples in the larger text. *Maniacs in the Fourth Dimension,* for example: this is Kilgore Trout's narrative about how people on earth with supposedly incurable diseases are in fact sick in the fourth dimension, and only there can they be properly treated. Sound fantastic? Vonnegut says no, offering (in silent juxtaposition) his own story of how an intoxicated Billy Pilgrim, trying to drive home drunk, fortunately fails to find the steering wheel of his car, even though he searches every square inch in front of him, from left to right, working his way methodically from the driver's side of the seat to the passenger's. Before passing out, he decides that someone has stolen the steering wheel. True? No: the answer is simply that Billy is in the back seat of his car. Fourth dimensions can be that simple, yet just as powerfully disruptive of our three dimensional lives.

Slaughterhouse-Five, published in March of 1969, was not only a best seller, but established its author as a celebrity spokesperson for key issues of the day. This shows how the book had to wait for the right times to come along before the writer could expect acceptance. An antiwar novel would not have done so well much earlier—not until the Tet Offensive of 1968 showed Americans how badly the war in Vietnam was going. A novel about an atrocity such as the firebombing of Dresden would not have been received as open-mindedly had not the recent revelations of U.S. atrocities in the Vietnam War, such as the My Lai massacre and the indiscriminate use of napalm, alerted readers to the fact that our side was not always above such things. And no previous era had been so concerned with youth, with a younger generation at once asserting itself so radically and causing so much worry among its elders. Not before had the country as a whole questioned its basic ideals, its sense of reality. Because Kurt Vonnegut's new novel raised these issues, it was the perfect book for the times, making its author an authority of sorts on the questions concerning so many of his fellow citizens.

Not that he had answers. Indeed his conclusion regarding the whole Dresden affair was that one could *not* write a book about it, could not even describe it as a scene in a larger work. "What do you say about a massacre?" he'd wondered, and decided the only comment could be the chirping of a bird after the smoke had cleared, which was what he'd heard that morning after the devastating raid on the city where he was imprisoned.

The bird, at least, was uncaged. For the next four decades Vonnegut himself would try to sing his way out of the cage that earthly life seemed to be. There would be times when he was depressed, and his work might show it. But for the most part he carried on, admitting that artists like himself performed the functions of canaries in a coal mine, more sensitive to poisonous atmospheres, whose own fragile mortality could keep others more happily alive. This sense of songful but personally doomed spokesmanship characterizes nearly all of Kurt Vonnegut's work that followed.

3

VONNEGUT'S
1970s

A Public Figure

As the 1970s began, Kurt Vonnegut—for so long an unappreciated writer, struggling to publish when and where he could—found himself front and center everywhere. From best seller lists and magazine features to widely reported speeches and commencement addresses, the man and his opinions were sought by an eager public. Young people were a natural audience, but so were their parents, themselves about Vonnegut's age and happy that at least one of their contemporaries had bridged the generation gap. It was no matter that the author dismissed his opinions as "wampeters," "foma," and "granfalloons," devices from the quasi-religion Bokononism in *Cat's Cradle* that underscored the self-consciously artificial nature of this faith. No matter because that was the essence of Vonnegut's message: not just that there was no absolute meaning to things, but that perfectly useful meanings could be contrived at need, simply if we were honest about the process.

The nonfiction pieces collected in *Wampeters, Foma & Granfalloons* span the author's transition from anonymity to fame. Reassuringly, what he says and how he says it remains consistent—it was this, after all, that had finally brought him fame, once the country was ready for it. But the later pieces appear in more noteworthy contexts. Fame did not discomfort Kurt Vonnegut the essayist, nor Kurt Vonnegut the public speaker. (For Vonnegut the novelist, it would be quite different.) A speaker or writer of opinion pieces is valued because of the credibility and usefulness of his or her message, and by the summer of 1969 the author knew people liked what he was saying and wanted more. He could start by mocking certain preconceptions about himself, such as his reputation as a science-fiction writer. Well, he did know something about science, but when asked by the American Physical Society to contrast science with his equally abundant humanism, he said the best humanist he knew was his dog, Sandy, who was more interested in people than anything else. Covering a space launch from Cape Kennedy for CBS News and the *New York Times Magazine,* he made fun of not just his scientific background but his present fame and fondness for an occasional drink by passing over the usual NASA promotional materials in favor of a children's book on astronautics.

"We are flying through space," he quotes. "Our craft is the earth, which orbits the sun at a speed of 67,000 miles an hour. As it orbits the sun, it spins on its axis. The sun is a star." And what does he make of this? "If I were drunk, I might cry about that" (78). So much for the pompousness of NASA's self-regard. But the anti-NASA position, that money for space would be better spent for needs on earth, is equally deflatable. "I flew over Appalachia the other day," he notes, adding that although the region's poverty can make life horrible down there, "it looked like the Garden of Eden to me." Why so? Because "I was a rich guy, way up in the sky, munching dry-roasted peanuts and sipping gin" (83–84).

His advice for dealing with such matters as science versus the humanities and NASA versus the social needs interests? In neither piece does Kurt Vonnegut give any direct answers. But his behavior during both essays makes it clear that understanding lies in taking a broader perspective, the lack of which has led to the problems at hand.

To college graduates he turns the table on predictable commencement advice by telling them that they are *not* responsible for saving the world, that the best thing they could do with their immediate future is to ease back and have a little fun. Responsibility will come soon enough, and, by being oriented to the joys as well as the tasks of life, they'll be able to do a better job of improving things.

To the audience at the rededication of a library, he says a few predictable things about the great wealth available in books and a few original things about the transformative power of reading them. But he then adds something strikingly original. Fiction writers may have done some damage because of this same transformative power, by relying on the easiest way to reach closure in their narratives, which is to kill off a character:

> We have ended so many of our stories with gunfights, with show-downs and death, and millions upon millions of simpletons have mistaken our stories for models for modern living. We have ended our stories with showdowns and death so often because we're so lazy. Gunplay is no way to live—but it's a peachy way to end a tale. It became more than the end of story after story to Lee Harvey Oswald and Sirhan Sirhan and Arthur Bremer, to name a few. To the likes of them, it became the most compelling myth, most ennobling moral lesson of our times. (214–15)

Hence Vonnegut's discomfort with having to write novels from a position of fame. Before, he might as well have been writing for himself, but now he knew how anything he said would be read by millions. For nonfiction that was no problem, as reality was unlikely to run away on him. But readers' imaginations were something different. Something imaginatively creative has a touch of magic to it, and definitely a life of its own. Who knows how readers will react to it? Knowing that so many *will* react is daunting indeed.

Breakfast of Champions (1973), the author's first novel written in the wake of his great fame, reflects these concerns. Its structure is, unlike that of *Slaughterhouse-Five*, a simple one: two narrative paths develop apparently on their own, but ultimately meet in a way that reveals thematic interdependency. But here that structure carries the burden of literary innovation, because one path, that of the writer Kilgore Trout, will intersect with that of his reader, Dwayne Hoover. Kurt Vonnegut superintends it all as a self-consciously present author, clarifying his own interests in the book's matter in a preface, but also appearing near the end to manipulate a scene for better dramatic action. In the novel as published, he also takes part in the conclusion, but only after some prompting—fittingly enough, by the book's first reader.

A consequence of Kurt Vonnegut's fame was having to meet people he never would have been involved with before. When he was up on Cape Cod, critics left him alone. Now, however, he'd been involved with several, including me, who became a professional acquaintance in 1972 (when I was assembling *The Vonnegut Statement*) and, over succeeding years, a friend. Critics working on him would turn up things (including a few essays for *Wampeters, Foma & Granfalloons* he'd prefer be forgotten), and—even more intrusively—ask him questions about them. This happened in my case with *Breakfast of Champions*.

Kurt's first gesture of friendship was to send me a present, "the kind of present only a college professor could enjoy," on the occasion of *The Vonnegut Statement*'s publication in February of 1973. It was about twenty pages of typescript (on aged yellow foolscap) comprising three false starts on a novel to be called *Upstairs and Downstairs*. Kurt did not date it but indicated that it was done a very long time ago, constituting his first dealings with what would become *Breakfast of Champions*. From the manner of its presentation, a narrator dictating the story into an old-fashioned Dictaphone machine, complete with instructions to the "operator," I could guess the pages dated from the early or mid-1950s. There was not a lot to it, just some characters who'd show up again in *Breakfast*, but it did suggest that the subject had been on the author's mind for some time. Now, in the 1970s, he had gone back to these pages when working on the new novel; that's why he had them at hand. And when that new novel was in production, he had no more use for them and thus could send them to me.

On my own, however, I'd found something more interesting. I noticed, among the acquisitions of a rare-book and manuscript dealer in California, a full typescript of *Breakfast of Champions*, finding it on a trip taken in 1972 in search of materials on the other innovators I'd been studying. It was amazing how much intimate stuff would appear in such places—kept, as it were, under the counter, to be offered to favored customers (I'd bought plenty of expensive first editions and other items by Barthelme, Sukenick, and the like). A dealer in New York, to whom I'd just given a good chunk for some signed firsts by Jerzy Kosinski, offered me a carbon typescript of Kurt's introductory materials, marked for copy editing, for *Happy Birthday, Wanda June*, which in 1971 had just appeared. A quick scan revealed several passages that never made it into the published version, so I quickly arranged for my university (at the time, Northern Illinois) to buy it, as it was beyond my financial means. Obviously someone at Dell had snuck it out of the office. The *Breakfast of Champions* typescript was more aboveboard, most likely a version of the work in progress being circulated in Los Angeles for movie options. This one I could afford.

Reading bound galleys of Kurt's novel a few months later, I noticed a major discrepancy: the endings of the typescript version and the galleys were completely different! Not just modified, but completely rewritten. As I had other reasons to phone the author about this time, I asked him why. He replied with a good story.

It turns out that Seymour Lawrence and his staff at Delacorte Press were anxious to get the new novel into production. Kurt, initially gun-shy at writing in the face of great fame, had delayed it longer than Sam Lawrence's business sense preferred. And so, because the Dell Publishing offices were right around the corner from Kurt's townhouse in New York, the publisher had hired a courier to pick up pages, chapter by chapter, as they were written and polished (Kurt's method, we knew from interviews, was to rework a page until satisfied, then proceed to the next). Turns out the courier was a Vonnegut fan (by this time who in America wasn't?) and had been reading Kurt's chapters as he carried them over to Dell.

Well, that had been going on for months. But this time, after the author had handed him the final chapter, he came back—empty handed (the pages had been delivered, as ordered) but with some questions.

"He told me that the ending didn't feel quite right," Kurt reported. The young man didn't know why, and at first the author didn't either. But as he thought about it, Kurt recalled a principle from his World War II combat training, about the rigors of bayonet practice (no pleasant task) and the necessity of "closing with the enemy" as a way of getting the job (however unpleasant) done.

"It struck me that I hadn't done this, hadn't come to terms with what the novel was forcing me to do," he said. Fame had at first blocked him, I knew. From the typescript I also knew how the theme and structure of what he did write involved facing the disturbing reality of having readers act on one's writing. But in comparing the two endings and asking why they differed, I was given the evidence that this confrontation was a major stage in Kurt Vonnegut's career, a stage in which he was not only coming to terms with fame but devising a way of making that new status productive of genuine innovations.

The original ending was a terminus of paths, but not a productive one. Instead, it was a dead end, with Vonnegut the author sharing ward space with his character Dwayne Hoover, the two of them confined to a mental institution—Hoover having read himself into this situation, Vonnegut being challenged to write his way out of it. Talk about a writer's block! For *Breakfast of Champions* to be successful, the author would have to write his way out of the book before it ended, so that his readers could be taken along—released, as it were, from the narrative.

Perhaps remembering the scene in *Slaughterhouse-Five* where Billy Pilgrim and Eliot Rosewater share quarters in a similar mental institution, Kurt Vonnegut turns to the same author they did: Kilgore Trout. But here it's a matter of Trout's work being done. As a character himself, he welcomes the release his creator now grants him, but he makes one last request: that the author make him young again. Were Trout a totally imaginary figure, that would be possible, just as easy as making the phone ring to move a character across a room, Vonnegut's trick from an earlier chapter. But in this case the task isn't easy at all, because the plea for youth comes in the voice of Kurt's own father. "How did I get so old?," Billy Pilgrim's mother asks him in *Slaughterhouse-Five*. As that question remained unanswerable, so too does the father's request here stay unfulfillable, except to help readers appreciate the volumes that simple silence can speak.

A special sense of silence, of awesome presence, in fact, is the ultimate destination of this novel. It transpires after the paths of Dwayne Hoover and Kilgore Trout have finally crossed. The former has been reading the latter's fiction, but taking it for fact, a circumstance that leads to mayhem and destruction—the very nihilism that a proper understanding of Kurt Vonnegut's own work avoids. Much of *Breakfast of Champions*'s bulk is spent in establishing these twin themes of writing and reading. Trout is followed from the East Coast into the Middle West, as he travels (incredibly humbly) to the Midland City arts festival, where he's to be honored as a great author. Meanwhile, in Midland City itself, the focus is on Dwayne Hoover, the details of whose life accumulate in a way that make him the ideal reader for Trout's fiction. The problem is that he mistakes it for fact. Early on, Vonnegut looks forward to when Trout will be awarded a Nobel Prize—not in literature, but in medicine, for his demonstration of how people are healthy to the extent that their ideas are. The pathological or beneficial power of thought, therefore, is the point; not simply imaginative creativity, but how it is used.

This quality of life, the very quality that distinguishes life from death, is self-awareness. To articulate the theme, Vonnegut introduces a third character, the abstract-expressionist painter Rabo Karabekian. Karabekian is another festival guest, and he too has things to say about Midland City's values (or lack of them). As such, he's the perfect complement to Kilgore Trout. For a culture that privileges the material over the mental, science fiction and abstract-expressionist painting can suffer misreadings and misunderstandings. Correcting these misimpressions lets Vonnegut make his theoretical points in an eminently practical way. When Karabekian speaks, it is not as a spokesperson for the author but as a flesh-and-blood character whose art has been mocked. His paintings resemble Barnett Newman's, and his philosophy of art follows Newman's as well: that a single narrow strip standing in an otherwise solid field of color represents life, the distinguishing characteristic of which is its self-awareness. Without such self-awareness, all is death. Needless to say, there are precious few distinguishing strips (Newman called them "zips") in Midland City, which is why Karabekian, Trout, and ultimately Kurt Vonnegut have work to do.

Karabekian, together with his theories of art, would later get a Kurt Vonnegut novel for himself: *Bluebeard*, published in 1987. In this decade the author would use the arts in all of his fiction; by then he'd settled more comfortably into his own artistic success. The 1970s, however, now continued with more public, even sociopolitical themes, reflecting Vonnegut's new role as an expounder of practical ideas.

Slapstick (1976), for example, restructures government according to the new social needs following the destruction of our present civic order. *Jailbird* (1979) looks to an actual restructuring of this decade, the Watergate scandal that disrupted the Nixon administration and government in general, by charting the fate of a civic careerist with roots in Franklin Delano Roosevelt's New Deal. During these same years Vonnegut was active as an essayist, the most important of these pieces being collected as *Palm Sunday* (1981). Throughout this body of work, all of which were best sellers and sustained the great public attention that had begun with *Slaughterhouse-Five*, the author's hand is quite evident. It's the shaping of the ideas, not just the ideas themselves, that gives them the appeal that had brought readers to Kurt Vonnegut's canon in the first place.

Palm Sunday itself exists as a testament to the author's acceptance of public spokesmanship as an important element in his art. His first collection, *Wampeters, Foma & Granfalloons*, was a simple chronology of what he'd been persuaded to save from the 1960s and early '70s. With this new volume, however, he works to shape it, being more selective but also arranging the materials so that they produce "an autobiographical collage," the book's subtitle (*Wampeters, Foma & Granfalloons's* had been simply "opinions"). And look what Kurt Vonnegut foregrounds as *Palm Sunday's* first section: "The First Amendment," four pieces regarding the banning of his own books and the general harassment of writers by governmental bodies. No wonder that his novels of the mid and late 1970s would have state institutions in mind when it came to the need for reform.

These complaints about censorship were first written to stand alone, but when brought together, they benefit not only from mutual reenforcement but from the "new connective tissue" (xvii) the author writes to make *Palm Sunday* less of a collection and more of a collage. He associates his political freedom to write with another factor, also under threat, which is his commercial viability. Vonnegut thanks his lucky stars that he's had either. Television had killed off his short story markets, and publishers of novels were losing their ability to nurture talent. Therefore, he reasons, he might be the last of a dying breed. How urgent, then, is the need to defend his freedom to write.

To the school board in Drake, North Dakota, that not only banned *Slaughterhouse-Five* from classroom use but dramatically burned copies of it, he writes a letter defending himself not as an intellectual or even an artist, but rather as a fundamentally decent human being not so different from the citizens of the rural high plains (he associates himself and his family with farm work three times, and he mentions his military service, Purple Heart and all). Vonnegut does remind the board president that words can be evil, but it's not the words that hurt—it's the evil deeds behind them, where the author is trying to direct attention for meliorative effect. His criticism is sympathetic:

> I read in the newspaper that your community is mystified by the outcry from all over the country about what you have done. Well, you have discovered that Drake is part of American civilization, and your fellow

Americans can't stand it that you have behaved in such an uncivilized way. Perhaps you will learn from this that books are sacred to free men for very good reason, and that wars have been fought against nations which hate books and burn them. If you are an American, you must allow all ideas to circulate freely in your community, not merely your own. (6–7)

Notice the recurrent emphases: community, citizenship, and above all a communal responsibility to group ideals. Such notions rebound through the futuristic *Slapstick* and the immediately contemporary *Jailbird*. In both novels the notions take life by being associated with an individual, Wilbur Swain and Walter F. Starbuck. So it is fitting that this letter to the Drake school board has an ending emphasis that is both personal and civic. "Again: you have insulted me, and I am a good citizen, and I am very real" (7).

Seven years later, in 1976, Kurt Vonnegut found that book bannings had become only worse. In this second censorship piece woven into the texture of *Palm Sunday*, he writes not the book banners themselves (presently targets of litigation) but the *New York Times*, expressing far less patience. He recalls the Drake, North Dakota, book burning, and remarks how "it was such an ignorant, dumb, superstitious thing to do." Yet his chiding is gently funny, finding amusement in the spectacle of school officials attacking artifacts: "It was like St. George attacking bedspreads and cuckoo clocks" (8). But the poor man's patience has run out. He's tired of being sympathetically reasonable. "From now on," he announces, "I intend to limit my discourse with dim-witted Savonarolas to this advice: 'Have somebody read the First Amendment of the United States Constitution out loud to you, you God damned fool!'" Of course, he knows that the American Civil Liberties Union will do that, that they will win, and that the book banners will be bewildered. "They are in the wrong place at the wrong time," Kurt says, adding, after a paragraph break, Wilbur Swain's mantra from *Slapstick*: "Hi ho" (9).

Just as "so it goes" was *Slaughterhouse-Five*'s dutiful utterance in the face of death's inevitability, so does "hi ho" serve both here and in *Slapstick* as a sigh of weary bemusement with humankind's occasional stupidity. Yet even a sadly winsome sigh can't mask the fact that, between the Drake letter and his *New York Times* piece, the political face of America had been scarred by the upsetting revelations of the Watergate scandal. In a free country, discourse itself should be free, open, and aboveboard, above all free from any tainting. Discourse regarding a presidential election needs this most of all. Yet it was just this that elements of the Nixon administration, apparently with the president's approval, had undermined. In 1979, the year *Jailbird* was published, Kurt

Vonnegut had this to say at an American Civil Liberties Union affair on Long Island, where a local school district had once again banned his work: "What troubles me most about my lovely country is that its children are seldom taught that American freedom will vanish if, when they grow up, and in the exercise of their duties as citizens, they insist that our courts and policemen and prisons be guided by divine or natural law" (11) instead of by the civic conventions our society has agreed to. Divine law is rationally unknowable, and not even the best physical or social science can authoritatively comprehend natural law. What happens is that both wind up being artificial constructs, but without the honesty of such artifice. Honest artifice exists in the civic contract, made up in response to recognizable needs and open to modification, by process, as those needs change. Just such a system is instituted in *Slapstick,* while *Jailbird* examines how one such system, FDR's New Deal, got turned by fraudulent appeals to God and nature into something as ridiculous as Watergate.

Well, as bad as the Watergate scandal was, at least we weren't being robbed of our freedoms like people were in Russia, right? The nature of this new take on an old saw, familiar from the cold-war years, prompted Vonnegut to end *Palm Sunday's* freedom-to-write section with a letter written to the Soviet critic and teacher Felix Kuznetsov, whom he'd met at a symposium in New York. Although their first conversations had been friendly, now Kuznetsov had compromised himself (in Vonnegut's view) by defending government censorship of some Russian writers. It was not just this censorship that bothered the American author, but that it was supported by Kuznetsov's claims that the offending writers were "pornographers or corrupters of children and celebrators of violence and persons of no talent and so on" (15), as Kurt summarizes. These, he explains to his Russian friend, were precisely the same charges brought against his own work. And so, with this fourth piece, the section comes full circle, with Kurt Vonnegut not simply arguing for the freedom to write, but complaining how opponents of that freedom habitually support their claims by vilifying writers in the lowest possible ways.

Civic spokesmanship, personal decency—for Kurt Vonnegut, they went together, especially so in the 1970s, when his own new fame coincided with a breakdown of so many civic institutions. In his comments to *Palm Sunday's* readers that close off this first section, he looks back on the Kuznetsov affair by putting U.S.-Soviet disagreements on writing in perspective. These arguments, he guesses, are predicated on "a desperate wish on both sides that each other's utopias should work much better than they do." As a result, "We want to tinker with theirs, to make it work much better than it does—so that people there, for example, can say whatever they please without fear of punishment. They want to tinker with ours, so that everybody here who wants a job can have one" (16), and so that rank pornography need not be tolerated. In practice, neither utopia works that well—no better, Kurt says, than the Paige typesetter that cost Mark Twain his fortune, which impressed him so when first demonstrated but never worked again. Yet such is the need for a better human life that utopians tinker on regardless.

Slapstick and *Jailbird* feature a great deal of such tinkering, futuristic and historical. Their protagonists are tinkerers: Wilbur Swain, a postapocalyptic president of a restructured America, and Walter F. Starbuck, a government careerist working from New Deal days through Watergate. But in each novel there is another tinkerer involved, and that's the author, Kurt Vonnegut, who writes autobiographically and self-consciously artistically in prologues that not only get the narrative moving but show an intimate involvement with the business at hand. Since 1966, with the introduction added to the new hardcover edition of *Mother Night,* the author had done this, defining the context for the stories of *Welcome to the Monkey House,* identifying himself as the creator of *Slaughterhouse-Five,* and explaining the necessity for *Breakfast of Champions*'s form. In these new novels, another dimension is added, that of the civic responsibility in expressing new ideas for the betterment of life. And for this, the prologues are instrumental in setting the terms of involvement.

"This is the closest I will ever come to writing an autobiography" (1), *Slapstick* begins, with Kurt presenting himself in the manner now familiar from his personal essays. The nineteen pages of material, almost 10 percent of the novel's bulk, constitute an essay, some of which involves the author's family life, some of which makes statements on the lessons learned from his family life that have generated the narrative to follow. First to be explained is the title. "Slapstick" is the comedy genre made famous by Laurel and Hardy, whose films, as mentioned previously, delighted Kurt during the Depression. Today it is what life feels like to him—life, with its endless tests of his limited agility and intelligence, tests that formed the plots of all those Laurel and Hardy movies. The joke in those movies was that the pair of hapless comedians always tried to succeed, struggling to do their best. And that's why the results were funny rather than just sad. "They never failed to bargain in good faith with their destinies," Kurt writes, "and were screamingly adorable and funny on that account" (1).

He notes that one approach Laurel and Hardy never used when portraying characters who are struggling with their destinies was that of love, not just because that was an easy way out (the staple of romance, not slapstick), but because they knew it would never work. That's the realistic side of slapstick comedy, and looking back over his own relationships with wives, children, and his brother and sister, Kurt appreciates how a little common decency always went a lot further than facile demonstrations of affection. Common decency, plus a larger basis for relationships: from the notion of his own biological family Kurt moves directly to his favorite topic of extended families, the more extended the better.

The profession of his brother, Bernard, gives Kurt the opportunity to expound on this subject, which will become the central theme of *Slapstick*. Close in so many other respects, Kurt and Bernard think in different ways:

> But, because of the sorts of minds we were given at birth, and in spite of their disorderliness, Bernard and I belong to artificial extended families which allow us to claim relatives all over the world.
>
> He is a brother to scientists everywhere. I am a brother to writers everywhere.
>
> This is amusing and comforting to both of us. It is nice.
>
> It is lucky, too, for human beings need all the relatives they can get— as possible donors or receivers not necessarily of love, but of common decency. (5)

With this emphasis on artifice, the author continues with a detailed account of a more naturally formed extended family, that of his own relatives in Indianapolis. The setting for this is the airline flight he (presently living in New York City) and Bernard (a resident since the 1940s of upstate New York, in the Albany-Schenectady-Troy area) are taking back home for the funeral of their uncle Alex.

We know from other accounts that Alex was Kurt's favorite uncle, a generator of much knowledge and also amusement. Here he's recalled for one of his key accomplishments, founding the city's chapter of Alcoholics Anonymous— another extended family. The fact that his obituary qualifies this information with the note that he himself was not an alcoholic reminds Kurt of how the newspaper was "preserving from taint all the rest of us who had the same last name" (8), as within the old conventions of social life such embarrassments as alcoholism or madness (or even a history of cancer) could make it harder for family members to make good marriages and find good jobs. And so even the biological nature of kinship among extended families is subject to artifice, to tinkering. Just as, in the Vonneguts' case, anti-German prejudice during World War I and the loss of their fortune during the Great Depression began fragmenting their strong base. After World War II there was not much to come home to. And now, in the mid-1970s, Kurt and Bernard were coming back—to a hotel, not a home—to help bury their last close relative.

A second point emerges from Kurt's discussion of his family: how his sister, Alice, was an ideal audience—for his jokes as a child and for his writing as an adult. He tells the story of her death from cancer (for an earlier society, something that would have been a secret, for the sake of the family's "good" reputation), just two days after her husband had died in the crash of the only train in American history "to hurl itself off an open drawbridge" (12), the stuff of slapstick cartoon humor but terribly real here, as there were children to care for. And so Kurt did, turning his own nuclear family of five into an extended family of eight.

Concluding *Slapstick*'s prologue, Kurt introduces his novel's narrator, a "terribly old man in the ruins of Manhattan" at a time in the future when the United States has become fragmented into rival kingdoms and the population decimated by a mysterious disease. "Who is he really?," the author asks. "I guess he is myself—experimenting with being old" (19). Hence the notion that *Slapstick* is "the closest I will ever come to writing an autobiography" (1), an interpretation borne out by the presence of another character, the narrator's sister, whose separation from him depletes his imaginative creativity. As president of what remains of the United States, he restructures society and its needs on the basis of artificial but functional extended families, identified by a common middle name (reminiscent of how wealthy families once identified their own). It is a good enough idea to generate another 220 pages of narrative, but its essence stands complete in the prologue, in which Kurt Vonnegut has quite practically outlined the most important elements in his own life, providing as much of an autobiography as any reader of his works would need.

Slapstick itself is at once the author's weakest novel while being, thanks to the prologue, his most compelling personal work. More compellingly personal than even *Slaughterhouse-Five,* although the brilliance of that novel's structure gives it a life of fiction that *Slapstick* lacks. For the Dresden book, Vonnegut had integrated his writing of the book with the reader's experience of reading it. *Slapstick* is more conventional, in the sense that Kurt Vonnegut as writer stays out of it except for the prologue. In fact he uses one of the oldest conventions of suspension-of-disbelief storytelling, by announcing that what follows is something he "dreamed. . . on the way to a funeral" (19). That's his job, of course, as a writer. While brother Bernard, an atmospheric scientist, filled the flight's hours by measuring the electricity in passing clouds, Kurt had closed his eyes and daydreamed the plot of *Slapstick.* Its theme and structure, however, had by this time been fully explained, thanks to the autobiographical nature of this novel's prologue.

Because of how the book was received, *Slapstick* occupies a special place in the Vonnegut canon. By virtue of the author's name on its cover, the novel was a best seller. But because of the weakness of its narrative inside—a step back in form from almost any of Vonnegut's previous works, with only *Player Piano* excepted—readers and critics were disappointed. This was precisely his greatest fear, the risk that had inhibited him from writing comfortably as a famous author: he knew he'd be read, with people hanging on every word, so to speak; and what if his writing wasn't any good?

By this time I'd come to know the man: I saw him in New York, he traveled to Cedar Falls, and the two of us kept in regular touch by phone and letter. He freely admitted that *Slapstick* was his worst book so far. But that didn't make the critical insults any easier to bear. "I felt like I was sleeping on my feet in a boxcar back in Germany," he laughed. But it was obvious that he still believed in the book's message. There was certainly nothing wrong with *Slapstick*'s prologue, which could stand by itself as one of his best and most important essays, itself using all the New Journalism's methods of fiction to report actual things. And so it would be in this manner that he continued, focusing even more on himself and his beliefs in the essays and interview that would come to form *Palm Sunday: An Autobiographical Collage*.

In March of 1977 I was able to witness his integration of fact and fiction at my own university, where Kurt spoke to an audience of a thousand or so. His writing has always been much like his public speaking, couched in the vernacular and especially engaging on a personal level. In books or in person, Kurt Vonnegut always worked in ways that brought writer and reader, speaker and audience together. He was doing this now in Cedar Falls, and both substance and method were identical with what he was writing at the time.

He started off with a question, involving his listeners from the get-go.

"How many of you believe that the great Eastern religions, with their marvelous depths of profound meditation, are superior to our Western styles of faith?"

Hands shot up everywhere. Didn't the famous author of such exotic works as *Cat's Cradle* and *The Sirens of Titan* feel this way himself? Guru that his readers took him to be, they all wanted to bond right now.

"Well, you're full of crap!," Kurt said derisively, shocking the many hundreds caught with their hands up. But as he signaled that this was a joke, smiling at their embarrassment, laughter filled the room, Kurt himself laughing the hardest. Then he gently, patiently explained how opening one's mind by reading a book was far better than letting it get lost in meditation. Yes, the Maharishi's headquarters was just a few counties away, down in Fairfield, Iowa. But the university's library was less than a hundred yards away and housed immensely greater riches.

Anyone who'd read *Wampeters, Foma & Granfalloons,* published just three years before, would recognize these sentiments from the essays "Yes, We Have No Nirvanas" and "Address at Rededication of Wheaton College Library." But it was nice to have the author himself reminding us now, especially in such a kind and sympathetic manner. Yes, he'd caught us off guard. But that simply made us part of the process, integrating us listeners in what he had to say, just as he'd done so many times in his fiction and would do again with the works in progress brought to the stage this night.

The substance of his talk, which lasted for over an hour, combined fiction and expository prose in a virtually seamless presentation. What made it seamless was Vonnegut himself, standing at the lectern and flipping through a looseleaf folder of material in all genres, materials he offered as cut from the same cloth. It was, after all, why he was there, and why over a thousand had come to see and hear him: he'd shaped his life as a creative response to a world needing better examples than our political, social, and cultural leaders had offered. Not even interviewers could get it right, he suggested, and therefore he presented parts of an interview he'd conducted with himself, now hilariously expressed in a comically different voice. Then back to some more essay material. Next, an excerpt from his novel in progress, presently called *Mary Kathleen O'Looney; or, Unacceptable Air* (published two years later as *Jailbird*). Finally, the chalk talk he'd derived from his second unaccepted master's thesis in anthropology at the University of Chicago, "Fluctuations between Good and Evil in Simple Tales," which for tonight's audience he reshaped into a critique of current national leaders (whom he faulted for not keeping the civic plot straight).

All of it was prepared material, but none of it was offered in a prepared manner. Instead Kurt improvised with it, moving from one source to another according to the mood of the audience, playing them like a virtuoso. And naturally the audience members loved being used this way. Everyone feels valued when being shown how they're of use. And here they were all part of a work by Kurt Vonnegut, created with their assistance in Lang Hall's auditorium.

Palm Sunday as a book is much the same as Kurt Vonnegut's speech that evening. The essays do not stand alone but profit from their company with others, a piece on how happy he was as a student journalist in college next to another memory of something happening just a few years later, how he "lost his innocence" when the United States dropped atomic bombs on Hiroshima and Nagasaki. The various essays themselves, existing as it were in a loose-leaf binder, are then commented on as the author flips through them; that activity is handled here by virtue of the interstitial material he'd written to make the larger work hold together as a collage. In a way it resembles the spatial juxta-position of so many fictive and factual elements in *Slaughterhouse-Five,* the lack of which (other than the basic contrast between prologue and novel) hampers *Slapstick* and some of his subsequent novels—until with *Timequake* another such integration could be achieved.

Palm Sunday gets its title from the author's sermon delivered on that day of the Christian liturgy at St. Clement's Episcopal Church in New York City. It closes the volume as if commenting on what the author has been up to in his novels, essays, speeches, and improvised performances. Has he been giving ser-mons? Not quite. Sermons are too often preaching to the choir, and, from his introductory comments to his audience at the University of Northern Iowa, it's clear that, if anything, he was prone to doing just the opposite. But just as *Slaughterhouse-Five* challenges customary notions about war (and about nov-els, war novels included), so too does this Palm Sunday sermon delivered in 1980 offer some corrective information on what we might have been thinking about one of Jesus Christ's own sermons, delivered to his followers on the eve of Palm Sunday.

Christ's subject that night was the poor, the subject that generated his famous statement, "For the poor always ye have with you; but you do not always have me." Vonnegut complains that for years, ever since his childhood in Indiana, skeptics would throw this line in his face whenever he'd express some pity on social issues. Was Jesus really being heartless, as socially uncon-scious as those scoffers who'd quote this statement in defense of their own hardheartedness toward the poor?

Vonnegut thinks not, and he devises his own gentle piece of instruction to show how. Could it be that Jesus is in fact making a joke, and that the point of his humor has been lost in translation? "In translations," Kurt reminds his listeners, "jokes are commonly the first things to go" (327).

To get Christ's message straight, the author reconstructs its context. It has been a tiring day, and what the Savior knows ahead is daunting: betrayal, scourging, and crucifixion. The crowds in attendance are "crazy to see Lazarus," just raised from the dead, rather than Jesus—"Trust a crowd to look at the wrong end of a miracle every time" (328). But at least Lazarus's sisters, Martha and Mary, are there, having in mind to soothe Christ's weariness with some pleasurably scented oil. *Expensive* oil.

> This is too much for that envious hypocrite Judas, who says, trying to be more Catholic than the pope: "Hey—this is very un-Christian. Instead of wasting that stuff on your feet, we should have sold it and given the money to the poor people."
> To which Jesus replies in Aramaic: "Judas, don't worry about it. There will still be plenty of poor people left long after I'm gone."
> This is about what Mark Twain or Abraham Lincoln would have said under similar circumstances.
> If Jesus did in fact say that, it is a divine black joke, well suited to the occasion. It says everything about hypocrisy and nothing about the poor. It is a Christian joke, which allows Jesus to remain civil to Judas, but to chide him about his hypocrisy all the same. (329)

Note the elements of Vonnegut's patented method. "Jokes can be noble," as he himself explains. "Laughs are exactly as honorable as tears. Laughter and tears are both responses to frustration and exhaustion, to the futility of thinking and striving anymore. I myself prefer to laugh, since there is less cleaning up to do afterward—and since I can start thinking and striving again that much sooner" (328). And look how the joke is expressed, not in the language of the King James Bible but in a common American vernacular as used by spokespersons who could communicate so well, Mark Twain and Abraham Lincoln. Elsewhere the author would add comedian Will Rogers to the list. Just as listeners and readers would add the name of Kurt Vonnegut.

What has Kurt's Palm Sunday sermon accomplished? He admits that as a sermon it is silly, but he knows the congregation will not mind. "People don't come to church for preachments, of course, but to daydream about God" (330).

These concluding words in *Palm Sunday* recall the ending of *Slapstick*'s prologue, where, after recounting all the interesting stories about his family, the author settles back to daydream a novel about how families do a better job of caring for people than do governments. Listeners in church and readers of this autobiographical collage are capable of daydreaming their own solutions to problems. Stimulation to freshly imaginative, strikingly original thinking is what they need, not preachment.

As for the decade's major political problem, the Watergate scandal, there had certainly been enough preachment. In its aftermath the country had turned to its most self-consciously religious president ever, Jimmy Carter, as an antidote. But even convicted Watergate felons came out of jail to mount their own bully pulpits, with Charles W. Colson preaching an expiatory Christianity and G. Gordon Liddy evangelizing for an even more vicious style of political action. Presidential aide John Dean became a celebrity by excoriating his own "blind ambition," the title of his memoir.

Kurt Vonnegut's daydream about Watergate, the novel *Jailbird*, begins with a prologue that serves as a sermon of sorts. Like the prefatory section of *Slapstick*, it is a lengthy and detailed meditation on an event from the author's distant past, in this case a lunch, arranged by his uncle Alex in July of 1945, with the industrialist heir and labor union official Powers Hapgood. Uncle Alex knew him because they were both Harvard men, and Kurt was being introduced because one of his first plans for a postwar career was to go into labor-union work, something the author considered a noble undertaking.

Powers Hapgood was noble indeed, not only following his father's example of sharing profits with workers but becoming politically active on national labor issues, to the extent of leading protests against the executions of Sacco and Vanzetti, whom he argued were victims of antiunion hysteria. His example was an important one to Kurt Vonnegut, as a young man considering career options and as an author recalling that meeting three decades later as America experienced another sociopolitical crisis. In 1945 Kurt was impressed. In 1979 he used Hapgood as a model for one of his novel's characters, Kenneth Whistler, as a way of introducing Hapgood's ideals into the narrative.

But *Jailbird*'s prologue is much more than that. Longer even than the generous essay preceding *Slapstick*'s fictional story, it moves from Uncle Alex to Hapgood to Kurt's father (who also shared the lunch that day, bringing to it an amusingly off-beat and fully irrelevant story of his own that quaintly characterized himself). Uncle Alex generates personal stories as well, and Kurt Vonnegut includes mention of his work on a novel about meeting his father in heaven, a project given up in favor of pursuing the larger themes of *Jailbird*. Hapgood's presence prompts the author to include short histories of major labor-union events—protests, executions, massacres—that set the tone for his character Walter F. Starbuck's fictional career as a civic idealist, the substance of the novel to follow. The prologue, then, is an autobiographical collage, much like *Palm Sunday* in its wide sweep of material, all of which comes to the point of making Kurt Vonnegut who he is, the person who when daydreaming about the Watergate scandal will come up with a novel like this.

Watergate did not happen by itself but was rather the climax of a long development in American political history dating back to the beginning of the cold-war era, at least. That's as far as conventional analyses take it, looking to the genesis of Richard M. Nixon's career as an anti-Communist crusader in the aftermath of World War II. Kurt Vonnegut's protagonist, who at the novel's start has just been released after serving a two-year prison sentence for his inadvertent involvement with the Watergate crimes, also took part in the anti-Communist hearings beginning in 1949—in a deft mix of history and fiction, the author has Nixon cross-examine Starbuck before a congressional committee. But Starbuck's career in government predates even this era, reaching to President Franklin D. Roosevelt's social reform known as the New Deal, which he plays a small but important role in implementing. That role is based on his own young idealism, a devotion to social causes similar to the kind Vonnegut's prologue identifies as the author's. Throughout his career Vonnegut would praise the civic institutions of his childhood that had worked so well: public schools staffed by the best teachers, available to all at no cost; social services provided with pride in their excellence; and a small well-trained and well-equipped army, existing principally as a defense force. How all this had gone wrong by the Vietnam and Watergate eras was surely demoralizing, and the task of *Jailbird*'s author and readers is to see not only how this happened, but how one can prevent it from happening again.

Is there hope for writing one's way out of this predicament? Vonnegut tempers his optimism by bringing back Kilgore Trout, made young again as promised at the end of *Breakfast of Champions* but now sentenced to a different kind of servitude, serving out a life sentence in a federal penitentiary for a crime he didn't commit. As a character in three previous novels, "Kilgore Trout" has been a figure for what Kurt Vonnegut feared he himself might become: a shabby, cranky, overlooked writer of low-grade science fiction. In the process, however, Vonnegut had become just the opposite, and so from his position of fame he recasts the figure. No longer is "Kilgore Trout" a neglected hack, because now that name is just a pseudonym for an entirely different kind of person: Robert Fender, a kind, thoughtful man given by nature to performing little courtesies for his fellow human beings. One suspects that's his motive for writing a Kilgore Trout novel about economics—and that the book will turn out to be much like Kurt Vonnegut's own *Jailbird*. There is much Robert Fender could be angry about, but he isn't, just as Vonnegut forgoes bitterness here (compared to the downright nastiness when economics became a theme in *God Bless You, Mr. Rosewater*). Fender, of course, is imprisoned; but so is Vonnegut, caged in the responsibilities of fame, for a crime he didn't mean to commit, never having actively sought such celebrity.

There have been times when Vonnegut was bitter, and Robert Fender has days like that too. But Fender vents such anger under a different pseudonym, "Frank X. Barlow," for more caustic narratives. For neither Vonnegut nor Fender are these contradictions, any more than was Jesus Christ's few harsh sayings, which can be attributed to his being "slightly crazy that day" (38), as would be any living being in a human body, subject to physical and emotional stress. In this way especially is *Jailbird* a practical, realistic book.

Jesus as a gentle jokester (as seen in *Palm Sunday*), Jesus as someone who by virtue of having a body that needs rest runs the risk of getting up on the wrong side of the bed some mornings—such references have been familiar in Kurt Vonnegut's work since the essay "Yes, We Have No Nirvanas," where the author regards him affectionately, as a welcome corrective to the Maharishi's market-driven economics. Note too that when Jesus appears in *Slaughterhouse-Five*, it's with another of the author's corrections, this time of the Christian liturgy. As it stands, that liturgy teaches people like the Romans only that they crucified the wrong guy, someone with connections; better to have the heavens open and God himself condemn Pilate and his crowd for killing just a simply decent human being—which is how Unitarians and Humanists, the author's own preferred style of believers, see the Savior. It is this restructuring of faith, and not Vonnegut's presumed obscene language, that gets *Slaughterhouse-Five* banned in conservative, fundamentalist school districts. But it is an essential part of the writer's method. Since the beginning of common-era dating, we have lived in a world whose ideals have been shaped by Christianity. And so if there is to be a readjustment, it had better include the principles of this religion—with any luck, retranslated and reinterpreted to be of better use. Speculative fiction, after all, is a fine way to do this, associated with religious belief as it can be. Remember that when Kilgore Trout is first introduced, way back in *God Bless You, Mr. Rosewater*, he's described as looking like "a frightened, aging Jesus, whose sentence to crucifixion had been commuted to imprisonment for life" (134).

In *Jailbird* the pseudonymous Trout shares prison quarters with Walter F. Starbuck, Vonnegut's protagonist tasked with making better economic sense of America than have presidents from Roosevelt to Nixon. For him Bob Fender's example is a good one, offering corrective vision on matters in the outside world. Starbuck's reentry into that world after his two-year prison sentence is dramatic, walking into the coffee shop of the Royalton Hotel (Kurt Vonnegut's own base in the city when coming down from Cape Cod to see publishers, editors, and agents in the 1950s) and finding a human support system more fundamental than anything government programs can devise. Expecting to be shunned as a branded public criminal, Starbuck hesitates:

> But I somehow found the courage to go in anyway—and imagine my surprise! It was as though I had died and gone to heaven! A waitress said to me, "Honeybunch, you sit right down, and I'll bring you your coffee right away." I hadn't said anything to her.
>
> So I did sit down, and everywhere I looked I saw customers of every description being received with love. To the waitresses everybody was "honeybunch" and "darling" and "dear." It was like an emergency ward after a great catastrophe. It did not matter what race or class the victims belonged to. They were all given the same miracle drug, which was coffee. The catastrophe in this case, of course, was that the sun had come up again. (123)

Here is how Starbuck writes in the manner of Bob Fender's Kilgore Trout, by defamiliarizing the familiar, only to bring it back in fresh awareness of how answers to our problems can be much simpler than assumed. Do we need a wonder drug? Well, the best one's right on the counter, fresh coffee. What's the biggest apocalyptic catastrophe we face? Morning! It happens every day, and every day we survive, thanks to such little common courtesies as practiced with such great elan in a midtown New York City coffee shop and in diners all over America. Vonnegut indeed has a manner not just of making it simple, but showing in such stark simplicity how the answer has been there along, obscured only by our weakness for making matters more complex than need be. What was the best definition for a chrono-synclastic infundibula? Just look it up in the current edition of *A Child's Cyclopedia of Wonders and Things to Do.* How to judge NASA's enthusiasm for space travel? Just compare it to another quote from a children's book, *The Look-It-Up Book of the Stars and Planets,* as Vonnegut does in his *New York Times Magazine* essay—and then imagine reading it drunk! From the many Kilgore Trout plots summarized here and in Vonnegut's earlier novels, we know this is just how good science-fiction works.

Walter Starbuck's ideals motivate his search for a humane economic system. As a basis, they cover all the key points, from the history of sociopolitical reform (and the persecution of its leaders) to an endorsement of such work by the chief reformer, and the most persecuted of all, Jesus Christ. Christ's Sermon on the Mount would remain a staple of Vonnegut's work. Here it is allied to a statement from *Jailbird*'s prologue, a reader's comment that love may fail, but courtesy will prevail. Much later, in *A Man without a Country* (2005), the author will chide the Religious Right and God-fearing politicians for their public advocacy of texts such as the Ten Commandments while overlooking the sermon and its kinder elements.

The language of that sermon is clear and simple, just like the statements in Starbuck's coffee-shop narrative. The sentences are simple, appropriate to the context. Both scenes—in the Royalton, on the mount—bear a metaphorical weight so gracefully that their messages seem natural and are easy to accept. The peaceable kingdom of every class and race; humanitarian service to people in need; the ongoing struggle of life, made liveable by the sharing of the most simple elements of sustenance—the human condition and humankind's fate are summarized in common words and comfortable circumstances. The simplest courtesy, Kurt Vonnegut has learned and Walter Starbuck discovers, can have the most profound effect.

A failed love affair dating back to New Deal days haunts the protagonist's life. Mary Kathleen O'Looney and a much younger Walter F. Starbuck had been unable to translate an initial sharing of interests into either a social program or a marriage. Did Walter betray her, he wonders? If so, it would be in a way that he suffered accusations of betrayal during Congressman Nixon's anti-Communist hearings and President Nixon's Watergate scandal: simply by innocent inadvertence. Forty years later O'Looney is encountered as an ostensibly poor bag lady, living homeless on the streets. In fact she is powerfully wealthy but worried for the effect of that power. With nearly half a century of modern American economic history behind them, the two can not only analyze the problem but solve it. Not money itself but the profit motive is what's destructive, whereas simple rituals (whether they be distribution of loaves and fishes or of morning coffee), especially when based on mutual respect, can be an effective way of keeping the business of life moving in the least destructive way.

The immediately practical solution to inhumane economics is the same that resolved the problem in *God Bless You, Mr. Rosewater:* Mary's fortune is broken up into a million parts and redistributed to the public. But there is a difference in *Jailbird.* Much of the rhetoric in the earlier novel was tempered by a suspicion of cynicism, or at the very least bitterness about money's effect. Eliot's famous baptism format, welcoming babies to Earth but emphasizing that "God damn it, you've got to be kind," could seem facile, even empty, given the lack of good examples. Good examples abound in *Jailbird,* requiring no more radical a change than heeding Christ's Sermon on the Mount or responding in kind to a coffee-shop waitress's pleasantries.

The language of poetry and small acts of kindness can indeed be transformative. Vonnegut shows this near his novel's end, when Walter Starbuck, fighting to control his grief at Mary O'Looney's death, makes some small talk with the ambulance attendants who've come to retrieve her body. They're Pakistani by nationality, and speak to each other in their native language, Urdu. For Starbuck, that's a worthy distraction:

> I inquired of them, in order to calm the sobs that were welling up inside of me, to tell me a little about Urdu. They said it had a literature as great as any in the world, but that it had begun as a spare and ugly artificial language invented in the court of Genghis Khan. Its purpose in the beginning was military. It allowed his captains to give orders that were understood in every part of the Mongol Empire. Poets would later make it beautiful. (222)

Kurt Vonnegut's own attempts to make language beautiful, and hence the world it describes beautiful as well, were put to rigorous tests in the 1970s. Like his heroes Laurel and Hardy—his "angels," as he called them in the dedication to *Slapstick*—he didn't give up, but strove to do his best in every circumstance. Not that he always succeeded. Ventures into drama and film proved only temporarily satisfying or ended up incomplete. In 1971 he published the text of his play, which had been presented on Broadway in fall of the previous year and run through a successful season, closing March 14, 1971, after 142 performances. *Happy Birthday, Wanda June* is notable for its redefinitions of heaven (a boring place, a turkey farm, as he'd call it elsewhere) and recharacterization of male heroism. But in his prefatory material, "About This Play," the author admits that his fascination with the genre was to combat loneliness, from his family having grown up and dispersed and his marriage ending, but principally from the solitary task of writing fiction. Drama let him share the company of actors for the better part of a year. He'd write in the morning, then see his work blocked out and read through that afternoon in rehearsals. Rewrites became something lived out each day on the stage. Even after opening he kept experimenting with the ending, making work on *Happy Birthday, Wanda June* a dramatic experience in itself.

But that was the problem: it wasn't life; it was only a play. And when the play closed, the cast dispersed, with the author back on his own once more. In 1972 he was lured into another project, a public-television special titled *Between Time and Timbuktu*. A pastiche of familiar Vonnegut themes put together by a team of writers for WGBH in Boston, the show served most of all to convince Kurt that film was not his medium. True, director George Roy Hill's adaptation of *Slaughterhouse-Five*, released that same year, is a cinematic masterpiece, but its expense daunted the author. Far better to stick to the typewritten page, where a change would cost not tens of thousands of dollars but a few dabs of Wite-Out fluid or the rub of an eraser.

More critically Vonnegut noted that everything of his put on film, which would include a cinematic production of *Happy Birthday, Wanda June,* remained one character short: himself.

In *Timbuktu's* preface he explains how he's always made himself part of his fiction, "so slyly" as to prevent representation on the screen. "I have become an enthusiast for the printed word again," he announces. "I have to be that, I now understand, because I want to be a character in all my works" (xv).

Being that character had once been easy. Writing as an unknown, "Kurt Vonnegut" from West Barnstable, originally from Indianapolis, carried no more weight than Paul Proteus, Winston Niles Rumfoord, Howard C. Campbell, Jr., or any other of his creations. Indeed "Kurt Vonnegut" had to be created for the man's fiction to work. And work it did, to the extent that by 1970 he was a famous figure in the country's mental life. For a time it would be difficult to work within that role, at once lonesome and spectacular as it was. Yet by 1976, in the subtitle to *Slapstick,* the author, having reembraced the printed medium, could proclaim "Lonesome No More!" And, throughout the decade to come, he wrote novel after novel about characters successful in their art, yet ever learning lessons that could be shared with anyone willing to listen. To Kurt Vonnegut's great relief, many people did, and were better for it.

4

VONNEGUT'S 1980s

Arts and Crafts

The 1980s were easier for Kurt Vonnegut, and—in a material sense—for most Americans as well. The cultural conservativism of the Ronald Reagan years was an antidote to the turmoil of the 1960s and the political mess of the 1970s. Certain 1950s issues were also put to rest, including cold-war terrors, plus—incorrectly, it would turn out—worries about militant Islamic terrorism (the American Embassy hostages in Iran were set free simultaneously with President Reagan's inauguration).

The Reagan years' answers were not, of course, Kurt Vonnegut's. Yet his own comfort ironically paralleled that of society's. His personal economy was good, his self-image strong. He had overcome doubts about his fame and the leadership it entailed. Compared to the anger he'd express over one future president's military actions in Grenada, Panama, and the Persian Gulf, and his absolute fury at another's in Iraq, Reagan administration policies were only an irritation. Vonnegut's essays of the period were rarely political, and by no means as social as they'd been in the preceding decades. Instead they addressed cultural matters; even his autobiographical pieces stressed his and his family's association with the arts. And the four novels he wrote in the 1980s emphasize that life of art as well.

Consider the line-up of protagonists. For *Deadeye-Dick* (1982), it's Rudy Waltz, raised in a family once well-to-do (thanks to ownership of a drug company that marketed quack remedies) and steeped in the arts (again, of a disreputable sort—the father's art-school buddy in Vienna had been Adolf Hitler). In *Galápagos* (1985) nature itself is the protagonist, directing a devolution of humanity into a species less dangerous to the world and to itself—but the narrator is Leon Trout, Kilgore's estranged son, who as a storyteller can work with the most fantastic, fabulous literary canvas of all. *Bluebeard* (1987) is given wholly to the arts and their impact on society, as described by Rabo Kara-bekian, the abstract expressionist whose theory of painting helps resolve issues in *Breakfast of Champions*. Then, in *Hocus Pocus* (1990), Vietnam veteran Eugene Debs Hartke narrates a slightly futuristic (by eleven years) story of a reshaped America—reshaped by economic and political pressures to be sure, but able to have its cultural history redefined in a more helpfully corrective way, as Hartke accomplishes by his teaching.

These are protagonists quite different from Billy Pilgrim, Walter Starbuck, and the like from Vonnegut's previous novels. Unlike those characters these are figures of authority—creators, as it were, of the new world being presented. All have self-doubts, of course. But so did the author. Like him they direct such interrogations to productive answers about life. And those questions involve central issues in Kurt Vonnegut's own beliefs.

From the start the author's treatment of issues regarding the human condition has always interpolated art and family. These two interests had been virtually divorced in the standard modernist approach. But, beginning with *Player Piano* and his short stories, Vonnegut drew on both his anthropological training and experience as a journalist to show how problems in family life could be resolved by a bit of imaginative creativity, while art itself could be helpful in clarifying the ways husbands, wives, and their children shaped more satisfying lives. This approach prompted him to write autobiographically of his own family and their experiences in art. Although not part of the customary prefatory material to *Deadeye-Dick*, Kurt Vonnegut's family story certainly stands fresh in the minds of readers, having been reminded of it as recently as the prologue to *Jailbird*, where Kurt's father is presented as innocently yet destructively distracted by aesthetics—by having an expensive saw blade wrecked by milling a beautiful but nail-ridden piece of old wood and, even worse, not appreciating the cost of his irresponsibility. Therefore when narrator Rudy Waltz begins his tale with detailed descriptions of his own aesthete of a father at work and play, questions about the author's core beliefs come up front and center.

Otto Waltz comes from a prominent family, is a painter and devotee of the arts, and a gun collector—three traits shared by Kurt Vonnegut's father. For the Waltz family, all three activities cause problems. Otto's art is not good, his aesthetic behavior is embarrassing (especially to an adolescent), and his gun collecting an invitation to family disaster, as the son takes a random shot with one of his father's rifles, only to inadvertently kill a pregnant woman eight blocks away. So much for the virtues of family life and art.

And no wonder these matters, customarily handled in an introductory prologue, are here made the substance of the novel itself. Therefore the first thing
to ask is what's in *Deadeye-Dick's* preface?

More material from the novel itself, that's the answer, presented here as the
author's commentary on title, format, locations, characters (including some
from history, others not), and the correspondences of all this material to Vonnegut's own status. It's a different sort of preface for him. Presented from a
position of authority, it signals his personal transition from the 1970s, when
fame was discomforting, to the 1980s, by which time he'd accepted and made
the most of what fame entailed.

As for the title, most readers will have assumed it's the same type of nickname the townspeople in the novel to come will give young Rudy Waltz after
he happens to shoot his victim (between the eyes, no less). In fact a *deadeye
dick* is more properly a nickname for a sailor, as the term refers to a rounded
wooden block serving as a receptacle and guide for the lines rigging old-
fashioned sails. But over a century later, in a landlocked part of the American
Midwest, it has been applied more literally to marksmanship. In Rudy's case
it's accidental marksmanship, just the opposite of good shooting—and so there
are layers of meaning just in the book's apparently simple title alone.

Next comes a warning that *Deadeye-Dick's* narrative will be interrupted
from time to time by recipes "intended as musical interludes for the salivary
glands" (ix), much as the line drawings every several pages in *Breakfast of
Champions* were visual treats. Those drawings also emphasized to readers that
the author was creating things, making things up, sometimes in the childish
manner of doodles. Here the recipes are similar reminders of his tinkering
creativity, for he warns that he's changed a few ingredients and manners of
preparation—and so, as for the etymology of *deadeye dick,* readers interested in
serious cooking should consult the originals.

Then some notes about Haiti, where the author and his wife visited and
where his character Rudy Waltz will spend some time. Plus details about four
painters in the novel, all of them real—one of them, most improbably but true,
Adolf Hitler. And finally an explanation of "the main symbols in this book":

> There is an unappreciated, empty arts center in the shape of a sphere.
> This is my head as my sixtieth birthday beckons to me.
> There is a neutron bomb explosion in a populated area. This is the
> disappearance of so many people I cared about in Indianapolis when I
> was starting out to be a writer. Indianapolis is there, but the people are
> gone.

Haiti is New York City, where I live now.

The neutered pharmacist who tells the story is my declining sexuality. The crime he committed in childhood is all the bad things I have done. (xii–xiii)

Only someone comfortable in his authority as a novelist can commence his work by breaking so many conventional rules of novel writing. Artists should not telegraph their intentions, tradition says, but rather let them emerge from the work, interpretation being the job of the artwork's receiver. Symbols are especially suspect, even when interpreted by receivers; for the writer to tag them as such is almost unthinkable. And autobiographical inferences are always off-limits, reductive as the making of such connections can be. In this case, the author wants such connections to be made. Or perhaps he knows that, given his fame, such correspondences will be drawn anyway, and this way he can better control them.

In any event *Deadeye-Dick*'s preface directs a reading of the novel, and therefore its textual penetrations of the narrative are important to note. The first chapter relates three important issues from the preface: family, art, and milieu. Family riches have destined Otto Waltz for a career in the arts, regardless of the facts that his artistic education has been botched, his native talent very small, and his painting style allied to the most hideous influence imaginable, that of Adolf Hitler. Otto and Adolf, fellow students in pre–World War I Vienna, both fail as artists; but look at their resulting careers! Vonnegut does not make the point directly, much less stress it, but Rudy's fate at the hands of his father's misguided aestheticism can be considered in relation to the fate of millions at the hands of Adolf Hitler. Otto romantically aestheticizes everything, making a spectacle of himself and an embarrassment to his son. Sometimes this penchant could be comical, if painful, as when pulling out all stops to celebrate the beauty of a young woman Rudy's older brother is escorting. Other times it is bitterly ironical, as in his support of Hitler as an artist (grandly purchasing a painting from his fellow student, most immediately to shame a critical professor but having the ultimate effect of saving Hitler from freezing to death or starving in 1910). Most practically, however, Otto's aesthetic romanticizing of firearms leads to Rudy's tragic mistake, making him the title character of a novel given to a life of near ruin.

So much for family and the arts. As for region, the novel's milieu, it is the city Vonnegut describes in his preface as a stand-in for the lost Indianapolis of his youth. Elsewhere we've seen these losses be of family and friends, but here the causality is culture. Culture had reigned supreme in Kurt's childhood hometown, but not in the Midland City portrayed in *Deadeye-Dick.* The matter comes up with regard to Otto's phony education, intended to be instruction in drawing and painting but, thanks to his lack of talent, a series of drinking bouts and whorings with a presumed teacher, a secret the two share: "Who else was there to detect the fraud? Nobody. There wasn't anybody else in Midland City who cared enough about art to notice if Father was gifted or not. He might as well have been a scholar of Sanskrit, as far as the rest of the town was concerned" (3).

What of the art he nevertheless did produce? In anticipation of Rabo Karabekian's critique of realism in *Bluebeard,* Vonnegut describes Otto's renditions as lifeless, with people, places, and things "looking as though . . . made of cement—a cement woman in a cement dress, walking a cement dog, a herd of cement cattle, a cement bowl of cement fruit, set before a window with cement curtains, and so on" (4). Looking back to statements on painting from *Breakfast of Champions,* readers might suspect that Otto's creatures show no sense of self-awareness. A dead culture produces dead art, we learn—not directly from this first chapter, but by interpolating it with what Kurt Vonnegut has said in the book's preface.

This death-in-life of misplaced aesthetics plays a direct role in the novel's major point of action, which is not just Rudy's irresponsible mishandling of the rifle but his father's reaction to the accident. Yes, Otto accepts responsibility for his son's act; the boy is only twelve years old, and has been given a key to the firearms room he should never have had, let alone the job of cleaning these pieces, a fascination that led him to fire a shot above the rooftops of his neighborhood. But the father doesn't stop there. Instead he stages a scene, dramatically destroying not only his entire collection of rare, priceless weaponry but the cupola from which Rudy had fired the rifle. Worst of all, he assumes that doing this for the police chief's benefit will absolve him and his son of punishment. That's how far removed from human reality is Rudy's father and his aesthetic life. And it's the son who pays the price for it.

Otto handles his own punishment like everything else, as a degraded form of opera. Rudy, however, is effectively neutered by this event. His family shattered, he discards any interest in sex, preferring to lead his life absolved from its consequences. His family riches from the bogus drug empire lost, he becomes a humble night-shift pharmacist serving customers in a poor neighborhood. But since high school he has, on the advice of a teacher, pursued a career as a writer, actually winning a drama contest and having his play given a performance (one night only) in New York—in the same off-Broadway venue, the Theatre de Lys, that hosted Kurt Vonnegut's own *Happy Birthday, Wanda June,* before it moved to the Edison Theater further uptown.

This becomes the second major point of action in *Deadeye-Dick,* in which much of the novel's second half is given over to descriptions of Rudy's play. Its title is *Katmandu.* Everything about it suggests it may be the same type of aesthetic escapism that ruined his father's art and their family life. Consider the motive for writing it. In the face of financial debacle Rudy has become, as a high-schooler, his parents' caretaker, as they have turned into virtual zombies lost in memories of their departed lifestyle and wealth. A sympathetic English teacher, with no great life of her own, notices Rudy's self-absorbed loneliness and suggests writing as a pastime—and then extravagantly praises its success, largely on the basis of poor Rudy having dreamed into existence his own fabulous world, his own Katmandu. Is this any better than his father's inconsequential art? Again, readers can recall what Vonnegut said in his preface about Midland City's inhospitable climate for the arts and how its empty arts center represents "my head as my sixtieth birthday beckons to me" (xii). Is Rudy Waltz's *Katmandu* a resolution of these problems or just one more facet of them? Again, interpolations of preface and narrative text invite such speculations.

Katmandu is a real place but is used most often in the literary arts as a gateway to Shangri-La, the magical land of plenty where there is no human aging. In Kurt Vonnegut's own young manhood, it was famous in fiction and film as the destination in *Lost Horizon.* The notion so permeated the era's culture that when in 1942 President Franklin D. Roosevelt was asked by reporters where Jimmy Doolittle's squadron of B-25s had come from to bomb Japan—actually a secret take-off from an aircraft carrier supposedly unable to launch bombers —he answered "Shangri-La," with his nuance perfectly understood. Rudy's play uses the same mix of fact and fantasy to make its point. It's based on the accomplishment of a local farmer named John Fortune—once a friend of Rudy's father, but alienated by the man's admiration of Hitler—who late in life set off on a new life of world travel, sending back postcards from exceedingly distant and exotic locations. The last of these was from India, the place where everyone back home presumed he'd died. "At least he saw the Taj Mahal" would become Midland City's mantra for appreciating his accomplishment.

In Rudy's play, however, his destination is Shangri-La, based on new evidence that John Fortune died in Katmandu, borne there on a stretcher in fulfillment of his dying wish. In terms of accomplishing the near-impossible, he'd reached his Shangri-La, a fact Rudy wished to celebrate in his play.

His father, though, had scoffed at the whole idea of such places of fantasy —a skepticism learned, by this time, at the expense of family and fortune. "It's all bunk," he warned Rudy, making an important distinction: "This is as much Shangri-La as anywhere" (114).

Is it? That's the challenge Rudy faces in living out his own life. On the surface Midland City would seem to be anything but a magic never-never land. But so were the stretches of apparently worthless acres the husband of Rudy's shooting victim bought with extra money from his lawsuit against the Waltz family, acres that he much later sold to the developers of Walt Disney World, a Shangri-La if there ever were one. Disney World is make believe, and everyone knows it. Its usefulness lies in what one does with that understanding, an understanding that had eluded Otto Waltz until it was too late. Too late for himself, but not for his son—or for the widower, who uses the Disney profits to underwrite his independence as a newspaper editor, writing fearlessly (and now without risk) on antigun and antiwar issues.

Rudy's own resolution involves his older brother, who'd been humiliated by his father's aesthetically mad spectacle staged for the young man's prom date. With a financial settlement from the construction company that had inadvertently poisoned their mother with a radium-soaked fireplace mantle (every such act in *Deadeye-Dick* is inadvertent, even Midland City's destruction from a neutron bomb, accidently detonated in transit), the two brothers purchase a hotel in Haiti, which they operate happily in conformity to that nation's law: that Haitian citizens are to be treated with a style of dignity apparent nowhere else on earth. What an irony, in one of the poorest countries on earth! But Haiti is also the only country where slaves mounted a successful rebellion against their masters and set up their own nation. It's no economic paradise by a long shot, but it is a system in which Rudy and his brother can function. And it also provides a satisfactory epilogue to their lives, long after their stories, the problematics of *Deadeye-Dick,* are over.

Two years after the appearance of this novel, Kurt Vonnegut published the most complete discussion of his own father that readers would ever see, an essay for *Architectural Digest*'s June 1984 issue, titled "Sleeping Beauty." It and several other important pieces would be incorporated into another "autobiographical collage," *Fates Worse Than Death* (1991), an important volume that with the novel *Timequake* (1997) makes a coherent representation of the author's 1990s. Elsewhere Kurt's father had been described as absent-minded and somewhat daydreamingly detached from conventional responsibilities, but in this piece he's portrayed in relation to his art. About architecture itself, the father can tell his son that there's nothing romantic, that it "had everything to do with accounting and nothing to do with art" (22). In a sense that's what in *Deadeye-Dick* Kurt had called the story of one's life. For his father, then, it had been a pretty flat one, nothing like the aesthetic exuberance of Otto Waltz's theatrics. But as for its epilogue, the left-over parts that happen only when one outlives the basic plot line of one's career, there is much more.

And that makes for a sweetly sad story all its own. Unlike other artists, an architect relies on clients to have his or her work built. With no enabling client, the designs might as well just be daydreams. Kurt Vonnegut, Sr., did have some important commissions early on, notably the Bell Telephone headquarters in Indianapolis (1929), but soon afterward the Great Depression and then World War II brought most major construction to a halt. As these events happened between the years when the architect was forty-five years old and then sixty-one, normally the most productive years in such a career, the man's professional life was gutted. So too was his family life, as during this same period his wife committed suicide, and new postwar conditions made it clear that none of his children would be pursuing careers locally (all three gravitated to work in upstate New York and on the East Coast). So his epilogue was an empty affair. But for his youngest son, a writer, it becomes something else: a story, once again the stuff of life:

> When I try to remember now what he was like when I was growing up and he had so little satisfying work to do, I see him as Sleeping Beauty, dormant in a brier patch, waiting for a prince. And it is easy to jump from that thought to this one: All architects I have known, in good times or bad, have seemed to be waiting forever for a generous, loving client who will let them become the elated artists they were born to be.
>
> So my father's life might be seen as a particularly lugubrious fairy tale. He was Sleeping Beauty, and in 1929 not one but several princes, including Bell Telephone, had begun to hack through the briers to wake him up. But then they all got sick for sixteen years. And while they were in the hospital a wicked witch turned Sleeping Beauty into Rip Van Winkle instead. (24)

That's a traditional fairy tale, amalgamation or not. Lovely, but unresolved. And so the son resolves it by creating an epilogue of his own: what his father, with his professional life over, was for Vonnegut, the son who when grown up would become a writer.

At the time of this epilogue, Kurt is still just ten years old, the Depression's onslaught having put him in the newly democratic confines of public (and not private) schooling. Here he makes new, working-class friends, "the ten-year-old children of the yeomanry of Hoosierdom, and it was they who first told me that my father was as exotic as a unicorn" (24).

Why so? Superficial reasons are that instead of donning a suit and tie to go to work, he remained at home in lounging clothes selected for comfort and beauty. A deeper reason is that instead of talking of business and politics, "my father was urging friends and startled strangers alike to pay attention to some object close at hand, whether natural or manmade, and to celebrate it as a masterpiece" (24–25). Whether his son's band instrument, a clarinet, or a moth he and his playmates had captured, everything was a marvelous object to be admired for its beauty. "He was the first planetary citizen my new friends had ever seen, and possibly the last one, too," the author concludes. "He was no more a respecter of politics and national boundaries than (that image again) a unicorn. Beauty could be found or created anywhere on this planet, and that was that" (25).

This is aestheticism, but working well. Otto Waltz's had gone bad, founded as it was on lies rather than truths. And there lies the difference between *Deadeye-Dick*'s problems and the solutions Kurt Vonnegut could fashion in his own life.

Art, including both its power and its danger, remained on the author's mind throughout the 1980s. Science interested him not as a physical report but as an arena for creation—for art, as it were. It's the same with politics and history; for Vonnegut, both are activities, and as human activities art is a necessary dimension, because human beings feel they must tinker with everything. As a bridge to these next works, it's helpful to look at Kurt's essay "Fates Worse Than Death," first published as a pamphlet for the Bertrand Russell Peace Foundation in 1982 and incorporated within the 1991 autobiographical collage of this same title as an example of the author's own tinkering with fate.

The piece is a sermon, formatted much like the earlier one that gave its title to Vonnegut's previous autobiographical collage, *Palm Sunday*. Here he's been invited to speak (or to preach) on the topic of nuclear disarmament, which from the Russell Foundation's program one assumes to be unilateral. Would not doing this put us at risk, Vonnegut speculates, making us all vulnerable to terrible fates, "fates worse than death," as his title puts it? Well, just what are fates worse than death?

The British, for example, call slavery just that, given references to it in their anthem, "Rule, Britannia." For Christians it's crucifixion. And so forth. For each example, Vonnegut deconstructs the logic supporting it—sometimes comically, but always with the underlying seriousness of America's own atomic bombings of Hiroshima and Nagasaki. Yet even there, as horrible as the deaths

were, dead was simply *dead,* no deader than St. Joan of Arc (similarly inciner-
ated) or the fate of anyone else who's only presently alive. Death is simply the
absence of life: "That is all it ever can be" (140).

Even life that evolves will finally be extinguished, the author notes, making
reference to his recent trip to the Galápagos Islands. But that same trip has
given him a broader perspective: "If you go to the Galápagos Islands, and see
all the strange creatures, you are bound to think what Charles Darwin thought
when he went there: How much time Nature has in which to accomplish
simply anything. If we desolate this planet, Nature can get life going again. All
it takes is a few million years or so, the wink of an eye to Nature" (145).
Humankind at present, of course, doesn't have stretches of time like that to
work with. But how might it survive another thousand years, certainly a meas-
urable amount of history?

To answer this question, Vonnegut looks forward one millennium to ask
our future descendants how they survived. Their answer is that they did it
"by preferring life over death for themselves and others at every opportunity,
even at the expense of being dishonored" (148). In this manner they will have
shaped their evolution in a benign way, breeding out the impulses of "Rule,
Britannia," crucifixion, "death before dishonor," and other destructive rhetorics. After all, it has only been the evolution of choices over the past thousand
years that have made these rhetorics so dominant, bringing humankind to the
brink of nuclear crisis. Why not just reverse the thinking? A better evolution
will follow.

In *Galápagos* (1985) Kurt Vonnegut does just that, giving his narrative the
requisite million years Nature needs to reshape the species in terms of the
choices it has made. The Galápagos Islands and a small group of humans isolated there by a apocalyptically destructive world war are the laboratory and
materials for all this. The narrator is Leon Trout—specifically the ghost of
Leon Trout, who was killed working on the ship that subsequently took the
crew and passengers on this nature cruise.

Galápagos is a much simpler novel than is *Deadeye-Dick,* just as *Slapstick*
was simpler than *Breakfast of Champions* before it—because in both cases the
author is simply working out the consequences of a thesis (devolution of the
species here, extended families as a social support system there). In this new
novel, humans slowly work their way around to the disposition of living at
peace with each other instead of at war. Food is all they need, and acquiring it
is quite simple. Absolved of the need to compete, they have less need of hands
and fingers to fashion advantage-giving instruments. Freed of having to think
so hard, their brains gradually shrink to the size appropriate to this new style

of survival. It takes a million years, but by the end humanity has become no more a danger to itself and the rest of the world than any other species.

Earlier, in *Breakfast of Champions,* Vonnegut had dwelt on the creative power of ideas, of how we are healthy to the extent that our thinking is. In subsequent works he'd shown concern with the effects of bad thinking. Therefore it's understandable that he'd make at least one try at removing ideas from the quotient, which is what reducing human brain size over a millennium can do. In the quieter American 1980s, in the wake of so much turmoil, disappointment, and fears for the worst, it's understandable that, within the relative peacefulness of the Reagan years, Kurt Vonnegut would be tempted to let humanity devolve into an even mellower state. Changes wrought by ideas could truly be maddening, as Leon Trout notes from his millennial perspective:

> Darwin did not change the islands, but only people's opinions of them. That was how important mere opinion used to be back in the era of big brains.
>
> Mere opinions, in fact, were as likely to govern people's actions as hard evidence, and were subject to sudden reversals as hard evidence could never be. So the Galápagos Islands could be hell in one moment and heaven in the next, and Julius Caesar could be a statesman in one moment and a butcher in the next, and Ecuadorian paper money could be traded for food, shelter, and clothing in one moment and line the bottom of a birdcage in the next, and the universe could be created by God Almighty in one moment and by a big explosion in the next—and on and on.
>
> Thanks to their decreased brainpower, people aren't diverted from the main business of life by the hobgoblins of opinions anymore. (16–17)

Is Vonnegut therefore abandoning ideas themselves, sacrificing the good effects Kilgore Trout had found within them, together with the bad? Hardly so. The term *hobgoblins* tips off his attitude. Scarcely a word used in everyday conversations, it is nevertheless known to all literate Americans and the phrase they are most likely to recall from the works of Ralph Waldo Emerson: "A foolish consistency is the hobgoblin of little minds." The twist, of course, is that Kurt Vonnegut is playfully suggesting that downsizing brains is one way of managing the effect of opinions, should the wisdom of writers like Kilgore Trout (and Kurt Vonnegut!) not be heeded. As is, *Galápagos* stands as a warning of what would have to be done were this wisdom disregarded.

In *Breakfast of Champions* the painter Rabo Karabekian argues his own idea of abstract-expressionist art, the notion that a thin band of light was all that was necessary to distinguish figure from field (as art critics would say) or human self-awareness from the rest of the world (as the artist himself puts it). By presenting Karabekian's position as a corrective to the bleakness of Midland City, Vonnegut privileges it as his own authorial view. That view subsequently faces challenges, but by the 1980s art (at least) gets plenty of chances to make life better. Abstract expressionism as a style is based on an idea—that the canvas is not a surface on which to represent but an arena within which to act. In essence it reminds viewers of where the action is: not in the world being depicted, but in the painter's act of painting (which is why some critics called the style "action painting").

In *Bluebeard* (1987) Rabo Karabekian gets an entire novel to himself. He's the narrator from the first page—Vonnegut having forsaken his customary autobiographical prologue or preface in favor of the briefest and most conventional disclaimer. He's the book's subject as well; it's his own memoir, not Kurt Vonnegut's. But there are links, the first of which is the story's Long Island setting. After marrying literary photographer Jill Krementz in 1979, the author acquired a second home, located in Sagaponack, part of the Hamptons area that had attracted several prominent abstract-expressionist painters in the early 1950s. Jackson Pollock did some of his most important work there, and one of Kurt and Jill's neighbors was Willem de Kooning. We know Pollock's life and the nature of abstract expressionist painting were on the author's mind, because in the December 1983 issue of *Esquire* he published an essay on these subjects, "Jack the Dripper," later working the piece into the autobiographical collage of *Fates Worse Than Death*. And so, living in the area, Kurt Vonnegut began thinking of these artists' contribution to American culture, just as he'd been examining his father's role as an architect, his sister's as a painter, and other allied interests. In 1980 he'd begin exhibiting his own drawings with a show at the Margo Feiden Galleries. And so, if there's an element of the author's own autobiography within Karabekian's fictive one, it's the nature of art and being involved with its creation.

A widower at the time of telling his story, Rabo Karabekian lives in solitude out in the Hamptons. Once famously successful, he's become an object of scorn since his massive abstract-expressionist artworks began falling apart because their paint loses its bond with the canvas (fears of Pollock's million-dollar works similarly falling apart in shipments to exhibitions were news items at the time of *Bluebeard*'s writing). And, in the novel's action, his aesthetic is being challenged by a new friend, young-adult author Circe Berman. Several of Jill Krementz's books were themed on young-adult subjects, such as her pictorial essay *A Very Young Rider*. Together with the fact that Karabekian describes his deceased first wife as having been an Earth Mother (much as was Kurt's first wife, Jane, who'd just died of cancer), these correspondences do suggest that *Bluebeard* is central to much of what was on the author's mind. His own fiction had always taken great risks, holding themselves together at the brink of deconstruction, and a decade earlier one, *Slapstick,* had indeed fallen apart. Or at least the critical establishment had told Vonnegut this while adding that it proved none of his work had any merit, as the author complains on page 104 of *Palm Sunday.* So while *Bluebeard*'s narrative is Karabekian's, key points in the painter's life match up with matters of personal and professional importance to Kurt Vonnegut.

At the very least Kurt and Rabo can be considered war buddies. Both have served in World War II, both given specific training based on their aptitudes (Vonnegut in the Army Specialized Training Program for college men meant to be future leaders, Karabekian as a specialist in camouflage, based on his experience as a painter). Yet both are thrown into combat as common infantry in the debacle known as the Battle of the Bulge. That's where each is captured and Karabekian seriously wounded, losing an eye. Most important, both end the war on the plains of Saxony in the aftermath of Dresden's bombing and the collapse of Germany's eastern front. This last experience is what generates Kurt Vonnegut's most important novel, *Slaughterhouse-Five;* in *Bluebeard* it will prompt Rabo Karabekian's most important painting.

Karabekian's professional roots even coincide with Vonnegut's, as Rabo's training has been with an illustrator of books, advertisements, and magazine stories, including ones appearing in the *Saturday Evening Post.* Those illustrations are accurate but wooden, and seem much like the petrified images put on canvas by Otto Waltz in *Deadeye-Dick.* The illustrator's personal life is equally wooden, its manners and values self-serving in a way destructive of other lives, including that of his mistress. She becomes young Rabo's friend and advocate, as Rabo has been the only person who treats her as a human being. In a similar manner Karabekian develops a style of painting more responsive to human awareness, a process that culminates with his and his friends' invention of abstract expressionism. Those friends read like a roster of the triumph of American painting, and so there is much at stake in his aesthetic.

Rabo's chance meeting with Circe Berman and their awkward friendship lead to the questioning of that aesthetic. Circe's own favorite style would strike most educated people as being kitsch, with overwrought depictions of sentimental subjects. It is no substitute for Karabekian's abstraction, which he defends as having the fluidity of time that simple rote representation lacks—

and also a truthfulness about materials that Circe Berman's Victorian artworks so exuberantly do without. But her questions about Rabo's parents and his past, together with the coincidence of his action paintings falling apart, lead him to reexamine a major scene in his life, the one he confronted on being released from a prisoner-of-war camp south of Dresden. Here, on the morning of May 8, 1945, he witnessed not just the end of the war but a virtual pageant of the humanity involved in it. Now, at the end of his career and near the end of his life, Karabekian takes everything he knows about the fluidity of time and truthfulness of materials and paints a huge work, covering eight of his older, deconstructed canvasses, that captures the essence of this scene, giving it the "pure *essence of human wonder*" (294) that his best abstractions had. More than five thousand persons fill the painting, and each has a story as interesting as that of Rabo's own mother, who not only survived genocide but happened on a fortune in uncut jewels in a corpse's mouth.

For each figure, Rabo Karabekian has made up a story before painting the person. Viewers, of course, would not know what it was but in regarding the canvas would be encouraged to make up their own story for the persons being viewed. This way both artist and audience are personally involved with the painting, their own human presence becoming as much a part of the work as any figure represented. The representation is not an end in itself, but a stimulus to action.

Such an understanding of painting's aesthetic is revolutionary, which is how abstract expressionism is understood in the canons of art history. Kurt Vonnegut knew something about cultural revolutions, as his first plan for a master's thesis in anthropology was to compare and contrast the Ghost Dance Society of American Plains Indians at the end of the nineteenth century with the new style of work being done in Paris by the Cubist painters at the beginning of the twentieth. One of Rabo Karebekian's friends reminds him of this same point, remarking how "every successful revolution," no matter in what, must have a core "cast of characters at the top" to serve as "a mind-opening team": respectively, a genius for new ideas, a well-regarded citizen who validates that genius's ideas, and finally someone who can explain those new ideas, whether they be Marxism, Christianity, or abstract-expressionist painting, to average people (199–200). For the last, Jackson Pollock is identified as the genius.

In *Fates Worse Than Death,* Kurt Vonnegut remarks that he got the idea for writing *Bluebeard* when *Esquire* asked for a piece about Jackson Pollock to be included in a special issue covering "fifty native-born Americans who had made the biggest difference in the country's destiny since 1932" (41)—surely the core of a cultural revolution that had created what historians were calling "the American century." Kurt had wanted to do Eleanor Roosevelt, but she was taken. And so, at the magazine's request, he looked into Pollock's life and work, and found this: that the breakthrough in abstract expressionism, as made by Pollock, consisted in not just laying on a stroke of paint, but after that letting the canvas do at least half the work. It's the success of this method that reveals how "there is a part of the mind without ambition or information, which nonetheless is expert on what is beautiful" (44). All without representation!

Of special interest is how Vonnegut takes this notion further, into one of his own concerns:

> And could any moralist have called for a more appropriate reaction by painters to World War II, to the death camps and Hiroshima and all the rest of it, than pictures without persons or artifacts, without even allusions to the blessings of Nature? A full moon, after all, had come to be known as a "bomber's moon." Even an orange could suggest a diseased planet, a disgraced humanity, if someone remembered, as many did, that the Commandant of Auschwitz and his wife and children, under the greasy smoke from the ovens, had had good food every day. (44)

To the *Esquire* essay Vonnegut adds this for the readers of his autobiographical collage: he doesn't particularly like Pollock's paintings themselves. Why not? "They show me no horizon" (45), which is what he needs, what his central nervous system needs, in fact, in order to properly locate oneself in relation to the viewing experience. Here is the author's own breakthrough, as expressed at the end of *Bluebeard*. In addition to their recognition of the fluidity of time, and in addition to their honesty in the use of materials, fully successful artworks must let their readers and viewers adjust to the horizon—in the case of Rabo's last painting, they must make it possible for viewers to create their own stories for particular parts of the work they're viewing, in tune with that work's larger purpose. These are the three areas of self-awareness Kurt Vonnegut has come to appreciate: that of the maker of the work, that of the receiver of the work, and that of the work itself.

Timequake, published ten years after *Bluebeard* and the product of the author's struggles throughout the 1990s, would be the complete expression of these elements, the equivalent of Rabo Karabekian's last masterpiece. But *Hocus Pocus* (1990) and one of the most important essays later collected in *Fates Worse Than Death* take major steps in that direction. Indeed they both retrace a much younger Kurt Vonnegut's path around Lake Maxincuckee, eighty miles north of Indianapolis, where for three generations the Vonnegut family had a little summer resort of five lakeside cottages. Across the water was a military academy, its order and formality (and warlike atmosphere) the antithesis of the peacefulness of a warmly supportive extended family on happy vacation. A lake is the location for *Hocus Pocus* and is the subject of Kurt's essay, "The Lake," appearing in the June 1988 issue of *Architectural Digest* and included as a key element in his autobiographical collage.

But there's much more to the correspondence than that. For each there is a geophysical marker that orients both central character and author to the proper sense of things. In *Bluebeard* it had been the horizon clarified by the flat potato fields of that region out along the farthest reaches of Long Island, where the fictive Rabo Karabekian lives. In Vonnegut's essay on Jackson Pollock, it had been the horizon not evident in that master's paintings that the author found so necessary for his own mental and physical adjustment and which the narrative of *Bluebeard* restores to the aesthetic of action painting. *Hocus Pocus* and "The Lake" have a common body of water, and both fictive narrator and actual author are soothed by it. But more crucial is its shape: a circle. Just as a horizon orients a person by stabilizing his or her nervous system, a physically defined circle (such as a lake) provides a rock-solid sense of security. Kurt Vonnegut had learned this as a child, when he could wander freely from his family's cottages and never lose his way, as simply following the lakeshore, tracing its circumference with its own physical action, was guaranteed to bring him back home. In *Hocus Pocus* both the circumference of the lake and the differing institutions on its opposite shores provide important reference points for the narrator (seeking his own adjustment) and reader (pondering the novel's theme).

Again, like *Bluebeard,* there is no autobiographical preface. It does seem that as the 1980s came to their end, Kurt Vonnegut was reserving such material for the personal essays that would contribute so much to *Fates Worse Than Death.* Instead the author uses the same technique that was so helpful for framing Howard W. Campbell's narration of *Mother Night:* an editor's note, signed "K.V.," suggesting how the narrator, Eugene Debs Hartke, ostensibly wrote the book. But then, on the book's next page, comes a combination disclaimer/dedication, indicating that this "work of pure fiction is dedicated to the memory of Eugene Victor Debs," the reformer whose motto Vonnegut had been quoting in nearly all of his speeches lately: "While there is a lower class I am in it. While there is a criminal element I am of it. While there is a soul in prison I am not free."

The narrative proper begins simply enough. "My name is Eugene Debs Hartke," we read, "and I was born in 1940." Gene Hartke, as he will refer to

himself hereafter, adds that he was named at the behest of his maternal grandfather, a socialist and atheist who, albeit just a simple groundskeeper, admired
Eugene V. Debs for his reformist beliefs and actions. So, two generations later,
the name Gene carries could mean nothing—except for the fact that as readers of a novel we know that Kurt Vonnegut chose the name for this character.

Gene's story takes place in the year 2001—eleven years ahead of the novel's
publication, but a relatively short space in the Vonnegut canon, which
stretches back to 1950 and (we now know) would continue accumulating
through *A Man without a Country* in 2005 and other essays and prefaces right
up to the year of his death, 2007. One of Kurt Vonnegut's fondest boasts was
that no matter how high or low his critical reputation, all his books were in
print—and widely stocked as mass-market paperbacks, no less. Few authors,
even living authors, enjoyed such a life for their works. Therefore the choice of
projecting the action of *Hocus Pocus* such a short stretch into the future invites
just the opposite reactions readers had to the million-year jump forward taken
in *Galápagos*. This new work was to be considered in terms of present-day
America, with an eyebrow raised to the considerations of just what might happen in the next decade were present trends to continue.

One trend of the 1980s was foreign investment in America—or, as some
commentators put it, foreign ownership. The cause for it was simply economic, rather than geopolitical: rampant inflation of the Carter years had, during the Reagan Administration and its towering budget deficits, driven the cost
of money sky-high. Domestic capital was stretched beyond limits; were growth
to continue, investments had to come from outside the country. As it did. But
the spectacle of Japan owning institutions such as CBS and Rockefeller Center was frightening to some, including Kurt Vonnegut.

Another trend was privatization of formerly public or even governmental
institutions. Here the lead came from England, where Prime Minister Mar-
garet Thatcher's Tory rule led to the sell-off of public utilities and the privatization of transport, including rail. In the United States this trend was more
common for services; a good example would be the cleaning and maintenance
of roadside conveniences formerly taken care of by state workers. Kurt Vonnegut disliked this trend too. In order to reinforce that dislike for his readers,
he combined it with the first one, and in *Hocus Pocus* a state penitentiary is run
by the Japanese for profit. For reasons of narrative structure, he places it across
a lake (in upstate New York, for fictive purposes) from Tarkington College, an
academy for wealthy learning-disabled students (a substitution for the Culver
Military Academy at Lake Maxincuckee, which in his essay Vonnegut suggests
had a fair share of disciplinary cases).

A third trend of the 1980s was wondering how to come to terms with the legacy of the Vietnam War, over for a decade. Veterans of it were finding it increasingly hard to fit into a society that had been ambivalent about the war at best, if not entirely opposed to it.

These three trends that Vonnegut projects into the not-too-distant future come together in the person of Gene Hartke, a lieutenant colonel with West Point training and notable service in Vietnam, who retires from the military to teach physics and music at Tarkington and later on remedial courses at the prison across the lake.

The first half of *Hocus Pocus* is given to Gene Hartke's career as a teacher at Tarkington College. His opinions could be considered controversial, but no more than Kurt Vonnegut's. He's fond of challenging his students' preconceptions, and he is close friends with another teacher who promulgates a radically revisionist style of history, such as suggesting that the Mexican general Santa Anna should be regarded as the true hero of the Alamo, because, in resisting Texas's War of Independence, he was simply trying to save this area, part of Mexico at the time, from becoming a slave state. Santa Anna as the equivalent of Abraham Lincoln? Ideas such as this, because Hartke expresses them to a naive student who is secretly tape-recording them for her father, an attention-seeking conservative political commentator, get Hartke fired.

In the 1950s Kurt Vonnegut had taught the same type of students for a time in one of his fill-in jobs when short stories weren't selling. Even more in common with Gene Hartke, he had spent the next three decades writing essays taking the same deconstructive approach as Hartke does in the classroom—not to mention publishing novels that got him in hot water with the same conservative forces that bedevil poor Gene. Yet here is the ultimate sign of the author's acceptance of his stature and belief in what he has to say, for what better proof of self-confidence can there be except to put one's ideas to the test?

The difference between them is Hartke's Vietnam service, against which the novel's larger themes (foreign investment, privatization) and actions (Gene's conduct and indictment) are played. Here is the greatest contrast between the two men's generations, as Vonnegut has Hartke explain:

> I read about World War II. Civilians and soldiers alike, and even little children, were proud to have played a part in it. It was impossible, seemingly, for any sort of person not to feel a part of that war, if he or she was alive while it was going on. Yes, and the suffering or death of soldiers and sailors and Marines was felt at least a little bit by everyone.
>
> But the Vietnam War belongs exclusively to those of us who fought in it. Nobody else had anything to do with it, supposedly. Everybody else is

as pure as the driven snow. We alone are stupid and dirty, having fought such a war. When we lost, it served us right for ever having started it. (160)

Telling students this truth about the Vietnam War is what Hartke considers to be the final straw in getting himself fired at Tarkington. By chance, the same day he's sent packing, he gets a job across the lake, at the penitentiary, teaching primary-level general education courses—the basics, as it were, to a population that had been denied them by socioeconomic and cultural forces in America.

Here Gene Hartke not only teaches but is in turn taught the underside realities of American life. He has come halfway around the lake to find it. Were the novel to stop here, it would be a simple social tract, just as if, should any of Kurt Vonnegut's essays stop with simply a complaint about their premise, then they too would be simple tracts. Instead Vonnegut's method is to come full circle. In his piece on the Maharishi, the author had begun with what he considered the flimflam of Transcendental Meditation (which had cost him seventy dollars), turned to traditional religion in the person of Jesus, but then come back to the flimflam and seventy dollars again, wiser for the experience. Gene's experience in *Hocus Pocus* comes full circle when a mass prison break develops into an assault against the college, an act that uncovers the sordid economic truths behind its operations. Economic truths and also cultural aberrations, for the social class that Tarkington College serves has cut itself off from the world's realities just as effectively as it has isolated veterans of the Vietnam War.

The lesson? A country cannot fight a war or operate an economy abstractly. That Vietnam and Reaganomics were indeed realities does not make them acceptable ones. Instead such disjunctures invite a virtual collapse of civilization, which is what happens here in microcosm. To clarify this point, the author includes a Kilgore Trout–like story, "The Protocols of the Elders of Tralfamadore," that Gene happens to read in the type of soft-porn magazine where Trout's fiction would customarily appear (as pulp between the pictures). Its plot is that extraterrestrials have infected Earthlings with germs that, within the Earthlings' large brain capacities, make them think they are the center of existence. Imagine the chaos that follows! Then pause to realize that this chaos is simply the status of human life to date. As Gene concludes, in the novel's last line, "Just because some of us can read and write and do a little math, that doesn't mean we deserve to conquer the Universe" (302).

5

VONNEGUT'S
1990s

Autobiography and the Novel

As a major American author still happy and healthy and writing for an appreciative readership in his seventies, Kurt Vonnegut spent the 1990s enjoying himself. There were still a few periods of depression, and even more of exhaustion; he'd often complain that he'd done a lifetime's worth of work and was ready to go home. But he'd always bounce back, engaging as ever. His autobiographical collage, *Fates Worse Than Death* (1991), is at once a deeper and more coherently written volume than is *Palm Sunday*. Bookending the decade are two other pleasurably self-attentive works, his collection of previously overlooked short fiction from the 1950s, *Bagombo Snuff Box* (1999), and the playfully outrageous accounts on postdeath experiences filed as a "reporter on the afterlife" for WNYC radio in New York, *God Bless You, Dr. Kevorkian* (1999). Yet, if these three works can be considered self-indulgences, the term does not yet exist to describe *Timequake,* except the one Kurt Vonnegut used to convince his editor that it was something legitimate if radically sui generis. With only the slightest bit of critical help, he called this new book the autobiography of a novel.

Fates Worse Than Death presents an author confident of his art and comfortable with his stature. Several of its component essays had been drafted in the 1980s, when he'd been celebrating the power of art in his novels. For the new decade, however, he weaves these pieces into an integral whole, not just adding filler (as Vonnegut had described his method for *Palm Sunday*) but actively thinking about how each element fits into his life. Readers can make connections too, noting that, by answering an interviewer's question that he'd like to die "In an airplane crash on the peak of Mount Kilimanjaro" (15), the writer associates himself with Ernest Hemingway with regard to going out honorably, famously, and fittingly. Thus when an analysis of Hemingway and his work appears a few chapters later, the parallels Vonnegut draws with his own life take on deeper meaning. Was Kurt putting himself in the company of a master such as Ernest Hemingway? You bet he was, just as in the volume's preface he not only associates himself with Heinrich Böll but mentions the latter's Nobel Prize and compared their respective ages. Proud of his membership in the American Academy of Arts and Letters, he nevertheless regrets its gate-keeping function and ability to shame nonmembers by their exclusion. Elsewhere he notes how Nobel prizes carry a cash stipend that history and economics have rendered far less grand than intended. Did he yearn for the prize? Perhaps. But as George Bernard Shaw informed the prize-givers when being notified, late in life, of his selection for a major award, he had already bestowed this honor on himself some fifty years before.

Kurt Vonnegut's writing of the 1990s does the work of an awards committee, so to speak: examining his contribution, measuring its range and depth, and then submitting a report for judgment—for the reader's judgment, the ultimate criterion for any award. *Fates Worse Than Death* does this, sorting through the materials of his professional life—not so much reprinting essays as reconsidering, reframing, and reintegrating them as an exhibit for the reader, who is spoken to in the process. *Timequake* is much the same, taking its own sweet time to become a narrative while Vonnegut, in the manner used for his autobiographical collage, picks up, examines, and comments on the materials of its making. Many of those materials are the same that he's dealt with in *Fates Worse Than Death:* not just Ernest Hemingway, but how the sharks in *The Old Man and the Sea* could be seen as critics (and how a neighbor of Kurt's at the time, a commercial fisherman on Cape Cod, explained how the old man should have filleted the best parts and stored them safely in the bottom of his boat); not just the American Academy of Arts and Letters, but how it becomes even more obsolete and irrelevant (and how Kilgore Trout, by discarding a manuscript in a trash can outside, inadvertently makes a contribution there).

These are items of a collage for the reader to consider. Such items work by juxtaposition. Unlike conventional narrative, collage relieves the author of having to say everything. Instead readers can study the selection and placement, then judge for themselves what the author is up to. Does Santiago's having lashed his huge fish to the boat's side mean he is a bad fisherman? No, just that he was more interested in displaying a trophy catch than in harvesting so many fillets. Have Kurt Vonnegut's own trophy catches of novels, so remarkable in forms never beforehand achieved, been savagely filleted by the critics? And the American Academy, "way-the-hell-and-gone up on West 155th Street in Manhattan" (as Vonnegut describes it at every mention, just like the repeated "so-it-goes" of *Slaughterhouse-Five*), is not so much a hurtfully exclusive organization as it is an accidental disseminator of Kilgore Trout's wisdom and the source of his fame. Is being pulled from a trash barrel how Kurt Vonnegut explains his own stature? He is a member, after all, and a very famous one, even though the fact that he's been admitted, and Allen Ginsberg too, seems amusing.

"If we're not the establishment," he was fond of asking the Beat poet, "who is?" Right here is the sense of Vonnegut's work in the 1990s. In previous decades he'd addressed his society's most common concerns, developed new literary forms, faced the challenge of celebrity, and paid tribute to the transformative power of art. If, by age seventy-five, he couldn't be considered a literary success, who could? The question then becomes what one does with this success. In *Timequake*, Kilgore Trout becomes a virtual savior of humankind; were he not drawn as so pathetic, so preposterous a character, Vonnegut could be accused of self-flattery. The truth is that the author, while far from writing social realism, wishes to remain engaged with the world around him, particularly a world that has come to pay him heed. Since 1969 readers had believed Kurt Vonnegut had something to say. And in the 1990s he was determined to say it, all the time remaining faithful to his art as well.

Because that art had disavowed representation by revealing its artifice at every turn, engagement remained a challenge. As an innovative novelist in the 1960s, Vonnegut could have remained in step with writers such as Robert Coover and William H. Gass by writing metafiction, fiction that explores its own being in lieu of other subject matter. But then, like now, the author had a subject in mind. In *Slaughterhouse-Five* he'd wanted to find the right way to portray the indescribable, to talk about the unspeakable, to put into communicative form the essence of an experience that by common understanding lay well beyond human comprehension. The Allied firebombing of Dresden in the final months of World War II was the largest massacre in European history, and because he was there, and survived it, Kurt Vonnegut felt the witness's duty to testify. But what could he say? Unlike his first five novels, there were no handy enabling forms such as dystopia, space opera, spy thrillers, and the like to contain it.

With *Timequake*, Vonnegut faces a similar problem. Postwar America, he sees, has not fulfilled its hopeful promise. Just as Ernest Hemingway had come home from World War I and found not a world safe for democracy but a civilization lulled by its own ignorant satisfaction, Kurt Vonnegut had returned from World War II determined to find out why people behaved as they did. Science wasn't the answer, and even training in anthropology was only useful for deepening his appreciation of the human spectacle—a spectacle he intended to observe and critique as a journalist, but turned out covering as a fiction writer. By the 1990s he was in his fifth decade of doing so, and—having been celebrated as a leading writer of his era—was wondering if the activity of producing a narrative could in any way relate to the condition of society.

Just as *Slaughterhouse-Five* generates a narrative by having the writer come to terms with his own rigors of engagement, *Timequake* exists not as a novel per se but as a work that tells the story of its own creation—not the autobiography of its author (that's *Fates Worse Than Death*) but of itself. Neither work demands a suspension of disbelief, but for this new novel Vonnegut makes a point of it. Quoting Samuel Taylor Coleridge on the subject, he credits this aesthetic as "essential to the enjoyment of poems, and of novels and short stories, and of dramas, too." But he then applies it not to literature but to the supposedly real world, and notes how that world fails the test:

> There is a planet in the Solar System where the people are so stupid they didn't catch on for a million years that there was another half to their planet. They didn't figure that out until five hundred years ago! Only five hundred years ago! And yet they are now calling themselves *Homo sapiens.*
>
> Dumb? You want to talk dumb? The people in one of the halves were so dumb, they didn't have an alphabet! They hadn't invented the wheel yet!" (88)

Were the author simply proposing these ideas in a novel, the effect would be fictive, but predictable. In fact Vonnegut as novelist is quoting a short story by Kilgore Trout, one of his characters. And so the fictive effect is squared. Then it's squared again, when the real-life author and his fictive character (also an author, remember) meet at a clambake and discuss the issues of their work. It is this exponentiality, which can tend to be abstract in the fiction of other innovators, that grounds *Timequake*'s reality. This reality is quite simply the making of the book, a process the reader replicates in reading it.

There's no illusion to it, and that's the beauty. Readers are not asked to suspend anything. Instead they're encouraged to augment the process by using their imaginations, making their own contributions to the work, just as Rabo Karebekian's master painting in *Bluebeard* invited viewers to make up their own stories about the figures depicted. This is, after all, what Kurt Vonnegut does with Kilgore Trout, coaching readers on how to reinterpret such basics about literary theory and the real world.

Timequake itself is rich with enfoldings, both of texts within texts and of writing within the world of the writer. The premise is a simple one: that on

February 13, 2001 (the fifty-sixth anniversary of the firebombing of Dresden, by the way, but not mentioned in this novel) the universe stops expanding, pondering whether or not to retract. As happens, it resumes expansion—but only after retracting to a point about ten years before. What happens is that life is immediately returned to February 17, 1991, where events of the decade are reexperienced in what the author calls a rerun of history. Temporarily robbed of their free wills, people are forced to go through the motions of what had already happened in ten years of their lives, until on Christmas Eve of 2000 the universe resumes expanding and "free will kicks in again."

As such, this fiction is Kilgore Trout's. But because Kurt Vonnegut had included it in an earlier draft of *Timequake,* which he is now rewriting (there's a timequake for you!), the narrative takes on new dimensions. Why so? Because the author makes a point of time-pegging his own action, dating it in 1996, as he's doing his rewrite of the original manuscript. Therefore, when talking about events in 2000, they are in the future, even though his characters have gone through this decade of history already. Which they have, in the novel's first draft. What's different in this second version, the version we're now reading, is that Vonnegut is involving himself in the rewrite.

That involvement takes many forms. Consider this: if *Timequake* were a conventional novel, it would be just a Kilgore Trout story, one more piece of traditional science fiction (and hence dismissable as fantasy, even worse as low-grade, disreputable fantasy for an underclass of readers). There's a parallel to *Slaughterhouse-Five* here, in that if that work had been written traditionally, it would have been just one more war story—and like so many of those, one that excused if not glorified war. Most important, because there are so many links, one should ponder how differently *Fates Worse Than Death* would have turned out had it been a regular memoir instead of the autobiographical collage Vonnegut makes it.

The innovative nature of *Fates Worse Than Death* is evident when comparing it with *Timequake.* At least half the material of this latter book, a novel, is similar in subject and manner of presentation to that of the autobiographical collage. And the autobiographical collage in turn has much the flavor of a novel: characters captured with great imagination, themes developed by means of imagery and symbolism, even the development by dialogue that in the hands of New Journalists qualified them as nonfiction novelists (or at the least as writers of literary nonfiction). There are even parallel techniques in Vonnegut's writing style, including the repetition of statements that, like the subtle repetitions of colors and objects in *Slaughterhouse-Five,* unify the narratives in an almost subliminal manner.

In *Fates Worse Than Death,* for example, the author relates Ernest Hemingway's suicide to that of George Eastman, who, after a lifetime that included inventing cameras and film, signed off, saying "My work is done" (67). Three chapters later, on an entirely different topic, Vonnegut mentions how the space-probe *Voyager 2* would come to an end by departing the solar system forever, giving it the epitaph "My work is done" (82). Sharp readers will remember the phrase as being George Eastman's; even sharper ones will note that the spacecraft had cameras, its work being to send back photographs of the outer planets and their moons. *Hydrofluoric acid* is another term repeated in different contexts: for a mother's suicidal moods (36), for an estranged wife's rancor (155). References to Kurt's war buddy Bernard O'Hare pop up all over, in many different ways, but managing to unify the book the same way elements in the author's life are unified, *when remembered*—as components in a collage. There are many more.

What holds a collage together? Two things. First, the artist's ability to select and join things in a meaningful way. Second, the viewer's ability to not just discern but also participate in that meaning. As is the case with *Fates Worse Than Death, Timequake's* structure relies on the abilities of author and reader alike to hold the work together. As in the most successful collage, the brilliance of the construction and the pleasure of its appreciation are measured by the distances these component elements can leap and still remain mutually supporting.

Consider the wide range of things, many of them happening on the same page, that take place within *Timequake.* Kurt Vonnegut speaks personally about the project, but he also tells many autobiographical stories central to his past, central to the person he became. He puts the novel's action in motion (the timequake and its consequences), but only for a few pages at a time; he always frames it with comments on how it existed in the book's previous draft, or where he expects the change he's undertaken to lead. He also includes summaries of stories (and occasionally direct quotes) by his character Kilgore Trout. He talks to Trout (and to others from his life and from the novel) assembled for the clambake cast party that celebrates the staging of Robert E. Sherwood's *Abe Lincoln in Illinois,* an amateur theatrical production that lets Vonnegut display some of Lincoln's most moving words.

That's a great deal to hold together. But so is life, as the author remarks after a meeting with author Dick Francis, a former steeplechase rider. Expecting Francis to be a smaller man, as a jockey would be, Vonnegut is told that "it took a big man to 'hold a horse together' in a steeplechase" (182). Well, what else is life but a steeplechase, and what else is successful living than keeping it all in a reasonable semblance of command? Those who can't, who lose their self-respect for this process, become suicides. Kurt himself confesses at least one such attempt, but he seems happy to have failed at it. As for the more integral survivors, who do hold it all together, he has immense respect.

Which is what *Timequake* is all about: holding oneself together through the steeplechase ride of life. Through its multiform manners of expression, the book not only warns of pitfalls and laments disappointed hopes but also offers suggestions for getting on better. They're all familiar: the support system of extended families, the practice of common decency, the transformative powers of art, and so forth. In one place or another, Kurt Vonnegut has said them all before. But here they are presented as key elements in a living, breathing work, a novel that quite literally tells the story of its own being.

Why does it exist? Because its author wants something better for us. And both *Timequake* and *Fates Worse Than Death* show how it can be achieved. Remember, almost every novel in literary history has been the product of components such as *Timequake*'s. But authors conventionally disguise their productions, relying on the reader's suspension of disbelief to cloak the mechanics. For Kurt Vonnegut those mechanics are the life of the novel, and in that life can be found inspiration for the reader's own. In similar manner *Fates Worse Than Death* could have been a conventional autobiography, with all the formalities that genre involves. But those very formalities disguise or obscure the best parts of a life, which are the processes of sorting things out. In his autobiographical collage, Vonnegut makes that sorting his major subject. Yes, much of the book consists of previously published essays and addresses, written for and addressed to widely various occasions. But one person wrote them, Kurt Vonnegut, and to both him and his readers that's what's important. Therefore his method is to integrate those materials with their ultimate source, which is himself.

In both *Timequake* and *Fates Worse Than Death,* the linkages of subjects are much like the workings of the mind: associative, meditative, and finally self-satisfying (in the sense of arriving at a sense of peace with oneself). Look at just the first six chapters of *Fates Worse Than Death:* they move, in this order, through his father's life as an architect, his sister's relationship with the father, the considerations of mental health this relationship involved, his mother's poor relationship with his father and her eventual suicide, the effect of that on him and his sister, his sister's art, Jackson Pollock's art, the lake where the extended Vonnegut family vacationed in a tradition that young Kurt hoped might incorporate him in the family architectural practice as his father's partner, fiction-writer and friend Donald Barthelme's status as the son of an architect, Ernest Hemingway (the son of a suicide) and his themes and techniques and own suicide, and finally Kurt's drafting of a new, more humane requiem liturgy. That's a lot of material for six chapters (of a 240-page, twenty-one-chapter book that has seven appendices as well). Within those six chapters, there are eight previously published pieces, but a great deal of new commentary as well—commentary that "holds the horse together" and points it in the right direction to win. *Timequake* has sixty-three chapters plus an epilogue within its 219 pages, and its materials jump all over the place. True, there are subliminal repetitions ("he's up in Heaven now" for every mention of a person who's died, "isn't this nice?" for every unexpected pleasure) and solid transitions (the ending of one otherwise variously concerned chapter will segue into the beginning of the next). But, as with *Fates Worse Than Death,* it is the integrity of the author who is producing this work that finally holds it all together. And rather than asking the reader to pretend that those efforts are invisible, the author makes them his own subject.

In both books Kurt Vonnegut infuses the narrative's making with a sense of himself, not just as the writer of it all (which would be simply metafictional, a stylistic exercise at best) but as an identifiable person with values and beliefs. In the best American culture, there is always a sense of such integrity being communicated. That's why *Timequake* includes Abraham Lincoln's speech, originally a historical record but used by playwright Robert E. Sherwood to encapsulate the man's deeply felt humanity.

Timequake ends with an epilogue that seems a reversion to *Fates Worse Than Death,* not because it's entirely given to autobiography (many chapters of *Timequake* are) but because it is shaped as a self-contained unit (probably why the author titled it this way, instead of as one more chapter). Usually Kurt has drawn on elements of his own life story in juxtaposition with his writing of the novel or with one of Kilgore Trout's stories; if the juxtaposition hasn't happened within a chapter (as it does for most cases), then it occurs with a chapter immediately following. But the novel per se has ended with a quiet moment at the clambake, as Kilgore Trout, announcing that his bedtime is near (what an elementary way to end a novel!), points out that the whole purpose of the universe, in all its immensity, is our awareness, a mental activity that can move faster than anything else, "a million times the speed of light" (213). Trout's proof is a simple one, having invited the author to look up into the night sky and glance from one star to another: light would take thousands or millions of years to pass that distance, whereas any person's mind can take notice of both in an instant. There's even a better word for it than *awareness,* Trout adds: "Let us call it *soul*" (214).

There is a transition of sorts in the epilogue, for it begins with news that a dear soul has departed this life on April 25, 1997—just four days before Kurt writes this page. Having finished his last draft of *Timequake* proper more than five months previously, he's indicating how this material is indeed an epilogue, standing outside the work. Yet epilogues comment on the work they serve, or at the very least serve as a test of that work's success. And that is precisely what happens here, in a measure of how well Kurt Vonnegut can further *Timequake*'s point.

What has been the novel's point? Simply that life can seem so disappointing, so downright crummy, because people (at their worst) sometimes live it as if they're on automatic pilot, just going through the motions of a lifelong timequake as if nothing really matters. It does; that's the message Kilgore Trout brought, first to the staff at the academy and in the end to Kurt Vonnegut himself at the celebratory clambake. In making that point the author has done more than create a character to announce it. He crafts an entire novel in demonstration, and he makes his own role in it as honest and apparent as it should be. Yet it's not simply metafiction; it's not just a writer writing, but a very real person doing the work, and elements of his autobiography have been essential (as the phrase goes, so accurately here) in fleshing out the voice behind the story.

Now, with all of this established, Kurt tells one more story, this time not just about his brother's death but even more so his life. What are the most fundamental elements in an autobiographical collage? Parents and siblings. These are the ones most frequently cited in *Fates Worse Than Death*. Within the writing time of *Timequake,* Kurt has had only one still living he could draw on, his brother, Bernard. And now's he's dead. But with *Timequake* finished, the author can draw on it for the strength (his own) and the credibility (his readers') to say the proper final words.

Final words are important. They not just honor the dead but allow the living to put things in perspective, to use their *awareness* (their *soul,* the Kilgore Trout of *Timequake*'s conclusion would say) to make sense of an otherwise senseless thing. Without that awareness, life can indeed be a depressing affair. But usually, if somebody, anybody, says the right words at a funeral, people can at least feel a little bit better. Tears make less of grief, Vonnegut had written years before, quoting Shakespeare. Words do not make more of grief, but give it an expressible shape—speaking the unspeakable, as it were.

And so when Kurt Vonnegut closes *Timequake* with final words for his brother, Bernard, he's doing exactly what the novel says we all should do: use our awareness, draw on our souls, and "wake up to do the important work that must be done," as Kilgore Trout implored people when the timequake ended and "free will once again kicked in."

Within the novel proper, there had been an occasion for it, Kurt's story of the last conversation with his first wife, Jane, two weeks before she died. That happened in 1986, a decade before the writing of *Timequake,* and so it qualifies as one of the personal elements of the novel's process, akin to the many references to Bernard Vonnegut, still alive. Because of a wife's prominence in one's autobiographical collage, the most personal to be added in life after parents and siblings, what's said here is important. Of crucial importance is that, after introducing Jane in the chapter (chapter 16), Kurt mentions that he did *not* say these words at her funeral. "I wasn't up to it" (116), he confesses. But now, writing what he insists will be his final novel—indeed, doing a second draft of it after the first one failed, a sure sign that the master's professional life is near its end—he speaks up.

It's a touching piece, a remarkable use of words to express the otherwise inexpressible qualities of grief. In tenor it anticipates the quoting of the words of another master of the American language, Abraham Lincoln, which are used near the novel's end. Like so many of Lincoln's words, they are simple, crafted for a simple occasion, not with pomp and bombast (the "bow-wow school of oratory" Vonnegut mocks so often, and that Lincoln's style helped bring to an end). That occasion is not the funeral itself but a talk the two had two weeks before Jane died of cancer, an exchange between "we two old friends from Indianapolis." The words are exchanged over the phone, but just as when read here, they speak warmly:

> Our last conversation was intimate. Jane asked me, as though I knew, what would determine the exact moment of her death. She may have felt like a character in a book by me. In a sense she was. During our twenty-two years of marriage, I had decided where we were going next, to Chicago, to Schenectady, to Cape Cod. It was my work that determined what we did next. She never had a job. Raising six kids was enough for her.
>
> I told her on the telephone that a sunburned, raffish, bored but not unhappy ten-year-old boy, whom we did not know, would be standing on the gravel slope of the boat-launching ramp at the foot of Scudder's Lane. He would gaze out at nothing in particular, birds, boats, or whatever, in the harbor of Barnstable Cape Cod.
>
> At the head of Scudder's Lane, on Route 6A, one-tenth of a mile from the boat-launching ramp, is the big old house where we cared for our son

and two daughters and three sons of my sister's until they were grownups. Our daughter Edith and her builder husband, John Squibb, and their small sons, Will and Buck, live there now.

I told Jane that this boy, with nothing better to do, would pick up a stone, as boys will. He would arc it over the harbor. When the stone hit the water, she would die. (116–17)

Kurt concludes by saying how "Jane could believe with all her heart anything that made being alive seem full of white magic." As such, she qualifies as the ideal reader for this aspect of her husband's work. The other side, its outrageous humor, the author had repeatedly stated, was crafted with his sister, Allie, in mind.

Did his words have the proper effect on her? He doesn't say, other than to credit her other beliefs, including religious ones not shared by him. But he's glad she had them. "Why? Because I loved her" (117).

Reading this in the copy of the typescript Kurt sent me late in 1996, I was moved, but also impressed at the risks he was taking, right within the living collage of his own life at the time. His children had never forgiven him for walking out on their mother in 1971, and his marriage to Jill Krementz in 1979 deepened this hostility. By no fault of her own, Jill became the odd person out in the remnants of Kurt's family collage. Would these feelings about Jane, not voiced until now, a decade after her death (the duration of a timequake, incidentally), make a difference with them? Who knows. But these words certainly would put Kurt at risk with Jill. Hard enough being a second wife, cast in the role of a wicked stepmother, without having your husband mooning over your predecessor.

With Kurt's typescript was a letter that had me even more worried—because he was worried that his editor didn't like this second structuring of *Timequake* any better than the first. Who knows, the discomfort could have been personal. The book was dedicated to Seymour Lawrence, "a romantic and great publisher of curious tales," and she certainly wasn't Seymour Lawrence. And Putnam's wasn't Delacorte Press and Dell Publishing. It was the miraculous discovery of Vonnegut's work by Sam Lawrence and then his almost-unbelievable dedication to it—publishing new books and reissuing all the old ones, keeping everything in print—that had made Kurt's popular success possible. These had been more than gambles; they were outright patronage, economically possible in the lusher days of publishing a quarter century before but unthinkable of the business world Kurt's new editor and publisher worked in now.

Besides, Sam Lawrence had never considered himself an "editor." Not even in the noble sense of Maxwell Perkins shepherding Fitzgerald and Hemingway and Thomas Wolfe through the rough pastures of publication, and definitely not in the proactive sense of editor Gordon Lish practically reshaping his authors' work into the minimalist fiction just becoming popular. Both styles of editing were intrusive on the artistic process, Sam believed. So he was not an editor, but a "publisher," as he insisted people call him. He found good work and published it, then supported his authors loyally. He'd done this with Kurt Vonnegut, to immense popular success. With Richard Yates, to critical success. But all that came to an end when Delacorte Press ended its agreement with Lawrence in the mid-1980s. Kurt stayed with the parent firm for one more novel, *Bluebeard,* but then went over to Putnam's. They'd done *Hocus Pocus* and *Fates Worse Than Death* with success. But given the author's own dissatisfaction with his continuing work on *Timequake* and his public statements about how he was tired of writing and wanted to quit, their worries about this strange new work were understandable.

It was a challenging book, as I found when reading the typescript. But to me, a Vonnegut fan for sure, the challenge was a delight. Its innovations were up to those in *Slaughterhouse-Five* (as the ones in his subsequent novels hadn't been). It struck me that the editor at Putnam's was trying to read it as a novel, which it wasn't. It was the autobiography of a novel, I decided, and wrote Kurt to this effect, taking the interpretive approach followed in this chapter.

Who was I to be advising Kurt Vonnegut? Well, if he hadn't asked for advice directly, he had told me of the editor's dismay. So it was her dismay I was answering.

My words to Kurt were of praise for the new form he'd devised. Some of this was voiced as lit-crit, though I didn't belabor the issues. Instead I tried to frame it humorously. He knew I was deep into baseball at the time, having (with a group of friends) owned and operated a minor-league club for the past seventeen years. So I phrased my comments as a manager would, visiting the mound to pump up the star pitcher working under pressure.

"Go with your strength," I urged. "Go with what got you here."

Kurt must have passed my letter on to Putnam's, or at least quoted it. Because in a few weeks he wrote me again, enclosing a photocopy of a new letter from his editor praising my approach. *Timequake,* faithful to the typescript Kurt sent, appeared the next September, its production delayed simply by the interval this correspondence had filled.

The book was indeed what I'd read, plus the epilogue. And this addition was a pure delight, for here the author was doing just what his character had urged him to do at the novel's end: use his awareness, his soul, to honor human presence in the world.

How does he do this? Like any smart priest or minister or rabbi at a funeral (they're trained for it!), or any articulate friend or family member (as people can become, thanks to good examples such as novels by Kurt Vonnegut): by telling a story about the deceased, especially a story of the speaker's own involvement.

The story Kurt tells is much like the one that begins *Fates Worse Than Death*. There it was about his father, including a letter of Kurt's that came back into his possession after his father's death—the pledge young Kurt had made in 1949, on the sale of his first short stories, to stay committed as a writer (26). Here, after a similar tribute to his brother's life and career, Kurt includes another letter, one returned to him by Bernie on his deathbed. Dated November 28, 1947, shortly after Kurt had begun work at the General Electric Research Laboratory as a publicist, it brackets the October 28, 1949, letter to his father announcing that he was getting out of GE for a more satisfying career in fiction. The letter Bernie retrieved, however, is a joke—a joke that nearly went bad.

The provocation had been another letter, one from Kurt and Bernie's uncle Alex ("Isn't this nice?") to General Electric, asking for a photograph of their up-and-coming atmospheric physicist, Dr. Bernard Vonnegut. Uncle Alex had been following his career with pride. He was proud of his younger nephew, too, but hadn't learned that Kurt had just dropped out of the University of Chicago's M.A. program in anthropology (where two of his thesis projects had been rejected) and taken a job Bernie found him as a publicist for the GE Lab.

What an irony that Kurt, as a brand new man on the job, would not only get a letter inquiring about his brother, but written by his favorite uncle!

If readers wonder how long their favorite author had been such a cleverly outrageous jokester, the 1947 letter proves he was in full form as early as then. After a pro forma response to Uncle Alex's request, detailing the provenance of the photo he mentioned, Kurt's letter takes a bold turn, adding that "Moreover, we have a lot more to do than piddle with penny-ante requests like yours."

That's how the second paragraph ends, perhaps knocking poor Uncle Alex out of his chair. The third paragraph, however, was intended to have him gasping for air, as he struggled to right himself on the floor: "We do have some other photographs of the poor man's Steinmetz, and I may send them to you in my own sweet time. But do not rush me. 'Wee bit proud,' indeed! Ha! Vonnegut! Ha! *This office made your nephew, and we can break him in a minute— like an egg shell.* So don't get in an uproar if you don't get the pictures in a week or two."

Imagine Kurt's joy, after two years of fighting World War II and another two struggling with an anthropology thesis and filing pool reporter's copy for the City News Bureau, writing what qualifies as his first piece of fiction. What fun he has with his material, even getting mileage out of Uncle Alex's polite gesture of enclosing token payment for the photo: "Also—one dollar to the General Electric Company is as the proverbial fart in a wind storm. Here it is back. Don't blow it all in one place" (217).

Imagine Kurt's joy, too, at making his favorite uncle laugh so hard, tipped off to the joke by the writer's signature, "Guy Fawkes." The problem was, by this point in his reading Uncle Alex was blind with rage, and didn't notice.

Imagine a furious response, then multiply it ten times. Uncle Alex not only prepared a letter of complaint to the president of GE, but hired a lawyer to get the rude employee fired. Thankfully, before any of this could happen, someone noticed the signature and tipped Uncle Alex off. This didn't make him any less angry, but now that anger was directed at Kurt. "I don't think he ever forgave me," Vonnegut recalls, "although all I intended was that he be tickled pink." But consider the dire consequences, sidestepped like a bullet:

> If he had sent my letter to General Electric, demanding spiritual restitution, I would have been fired. I don't know what would then have become of me and my wife and son. Nor would I have ever come upon the material for my novels *Player Piano* and *Cat's Cradle,* and several short stories.
>
> Uncle Alex gave Bernie the Guy Fawkes letter. Bernie on his deathbed gave it to me. Otherwise, it would have been lost forever. But there it is.
>
> Timequake! I'm back in 1947 again, having just come to work for General Electric, and a rerun begins. We all have to do again exactly what we did the first time through, for good or ill. (218)

As for some last words on Bernard Vonnegut, words that end *Timequake,* Kurt finds them with a woman "who knew Bernie only for the last ten days of his life, in the hospice at St. Peter's Hospital in Albany." She described his manners (while dying!) as "courtly" and "elegant."

These were the qualities that had struck me when meeting Dr. Vonnegut at the State University of New York–Albany twenty-one years before. What a brother, indeed!

Or, as Kurt concludes his epilogue, "What a language" (219).

Encouraging Kurt Vonnegut to publish something is satisfying, but no special deal. John Somer and I had success in getting him to collect the essays of

Wampeters, Foma & Granfalloons, and saying those corny words about going with his best stuff and sticking to what got him here surely meant no more than the other goofy things baseball people say out there on the mound—a mound that by the rules is one single person's domain.

More special is Peter Reed's success in convincing Kurt that the stories passed over in 1968 for *Welcome to the Monkey House* should be reprinted. That was a tougher one, because John and I had thought we had him talked into that too, as part of *Wampeters, Foma & Granfalloons.* He was specific then about the rejection: they'd been culled not just in 1968 but from his paperback collection, *Canary in a Cat House,* back in 1961. There would be no third-time lucky charm to our attempt in 1974, and the world's surely better for that— because in 1999, as the fifth decade of Kurt Vonnegut's long career was coming to a close, Peter not only got the stories in print but provided the occasion for their author to write important new commentary.

Those old letters of Kurt's that frame *Fates Worse Than Death* and *Timequake,* the tidying up he does of certain issues (last words for Jane, a decent exit for Kilgore Trout), the self-appraisal of his life and its concerns—this general sense of putting things in order that characterizes Vonnegut's 1990s is present in the introduction and the coda that he wrote for *Bagombo Snuff Box: Uncollected Short Fiction* (1999). The golden age of American magazine fiction, beginning shortly after the turn of the century, is recalled—fondly for its heyday and somewhat sardonically for the fact that it had just about ten more years of life when Kurt Vonnegut signed on as a short story writer. In 1950, he notes, he expected to be at it the rest of his life. That it mostly petered out while he was just getting established isn't lamented (although the loss of the short story's world of support is). Instead, by 1999 Kurt can put it in perspective. He could have died in Dresden, for that matter—nearly everyone else there did! He could have landed a job as a journalist, his career of choice in 1945—but returning vets and experienced women had claim to all the positions. So he studied anthropology—not for a career in academics, to be sure, but to enrich his knowledge of humankind should any opportunities at newspapers open up.

They didn't. Plus his professors at the University of Chicago bounced him out, rejecting his claims (in an M.A. thesis) that similarities between leaders of the Cubist movement and Plains Indians uprisings could not be ignored. He was being unprofessional in his approach, they pointed out; anthropology as practiced in the 1940s did not yet countenance the comparison of civilized and primitive groups.

So anthropology hadn't worked out. Neither did writing publicity for the General Electric Research Laboratory. Had any of these career paths been satisfying and productive—or even possible—Kurt Vonnegut would never have become a short story writer for the family magazines. Therefore, when this career option dissolved as well, he could now see, from the perspective of 1999, that it was just as well. The world had something else in mind for Kurt Vonnegut.

Knowing both the man's social philosophy and at this late stage his literary history as well, we can say that his talents were needed elsewhere. From that phony letter to his uncle Alex that ends *Timequake,* we know at once that his literary talents were both immense and going to waste (if not being downright self-destructive) at GE. But were his family-magazine stories of the 1950s *not* useful? True, his subsequent novels were much bigger fish to fry, and were given the opportunity of having great cultural effect. But are the stories like these being gathered together and reprinted now of no consequence? In 1961, 1968, and 1974 he'd thought so, we know. So what's the reason to save them now, these remnants from one of several career paths that couldn't be sustained?

The answer comes in what Vonnegut offers next, his rules for creative writing, a subject he has taught both in anonymity and fame. There are eight, and most seem reasonable enough: don't waste the readers' time, give them at least one character they can root for, give that character a desire, always advance the action, don't start too far away from that action's resolution, put that character to a test, and keep your audience, ideally just the one person who'll be reading your fiction at one time, in mind all the time. More interesting, and more original to Kurt Vonnegut's own work, is the eighth:

> Give your readers as much information as possible as soon as possible. To heck with suspense. Readers should have such complete understanding of what is going on, where and why, that they could finish the story themselves, should cockroaches eat the last few pages. (10)

Is this a reduction to formula? *Collier's* and the *Saturday Evening Post* certainly demanded them, but not in the reductivist way academic critics might suppose. As a trained anthropologist and sharply attentive observer of his society, Kurt Vonnegut knew from the start of his fiction-writing career that people not only respond to structures but need them to make sense of things, to feel comfortable with what's being encountered. Within those structures—within "boundaries like a playing field," as Kurt now puts it—there can be surprises, but always in a way that, in retrospect, can be seen to have fit. "The story simply can't go anywhere," he insists, and neither can a novel:

This, I feel, invites readers to come off the sidelines, to get into the game with the author. Where is the story going next? Where should it go? No fair! Hopeless situation! Touchdown!

Remember my rule number eight? "Give your readers as much information as soon as possible"? That's so they can play along. Where, outside the Groves of Academe, does anybody like a story where so much information is withheld or arcane that there is no way for readers to play along? (11)

There, in a nutshell, is the secret to this author's success. His surprises have been the most radical in recent literary history, but they've been successful because they allow the reader to play along. And when the story's done, they admit that even if they were fooled for a while, the author has played fairly with them, within the boundaries of their shared culture—within the structures of their common existence.

Kurt Vonnegut ends the 1990s, his last complete and fully productive decade, with a little play of the spirit called *God Bless You, Dr. Kevorkian* (1999). Ostensibly a series of near-death accounts from "WNYC's reporter on the afterlife" (7), it consists of twenty-one brief segments (originally broadcast on New York public radio) that do exactly what the author says pieces of fiction should do: give the readers all the information they need, but surprise them with new twists and turns, always within the rules of the game, so that they can enjoyably play along.

The rules are stated in the volume's introduction. One premise, that of near-death experiences recounted by people revived at the last moment in last-ditch medical operations, is combined with another, the assisted suicides supervised by Dr. Jack Kevorkian. Both were prominent news items of the time. By putting them together, Vonnegut creates a credible (if whimsical) situation in which, with the cooperation of Dr. Kevorkian and the criminal execution staff at the Texas State Penitentiary (a third news item of the day), he is brought to death's door, and then he is revived, so that he can report on what he has seen.

What's seen are twenty-one subjects from the past and the recent present: Sir Isaac Newton, curious even in the afterlife about new discoveries on Earth; William Shakespeare, who responds to the interviewer's Geraldo Rivera–like questions with famous lines from his plays; assassin James Earl Ray, and so forth. The routine turns out to be deflationary, as his subjects are either hopelessly banal or ridiculously deluded. As a theme, it fits Vonnegut's notions of the afterlife that he'd voiced in the 1970s, in *Happy Birthday, Wanda June* and *Slapstick:* that this life here on Earth is the best we'll ever have, that even the rewards of heaven are puny compared to the riches now available. Even Adolf Hitler, whom one would presume to be suffering in eternity, comes across like a smug politician, expressing "remorse for any actions of his, however indirectly, which might have had anything to do with the violent deaths suffered by thirty-five million people during World War II" (45). The führer reminds Kurt that he and Eva had perished as well; they too were victims.

With this little bit of 1990s shallowness Kurt Vonnegut makes his point. And he makes it in an appropriate way, acknowledging that, at his age, everything that happens to him is a near-death experience.

As happens, Kurt would have five more years on Earth. The events of the next decade, as many of them as he had time for, would stir him into more writerly action than he'd taken in many years. Whereas much of his 1990s work had been quietly appreciative of his own life and work, celebrating his midwestern roots by quoting Sir Walter Scott in the coda to *Bagombo Snuff Box* that "Breathes there the man, with soul so dead, who never to himself has said, this is my own, my native land!," the years 2000–2005 were so trying that, in his last book published in his lifetime, he declared himself a man without a country.

Yet that country, beleaguered as it was in those years, was not yet without Kurt Vonnegut. *A Man without a Country* would make the most of this fact.

CONCLUSION

Vonnegut Uncaged

Kurt Vonnegut had stayed active late in life because, in all humility, he felt his country needed him. Or at least that he could be of use, which we know was the cardinal value he believed human beings could possess.

Before *Slaughterhouse-Five* brought him fame, and even celebrity, he'd given lectures when and where he could—mostly as a source of income, but also because he believed he had good advice to share. Throughout the next three decades he continued speaking, well after any need to generate income or promote the sale of books. In the years 2000–2007—into his eighties, no less—he was still making ten major lecture appearances per year. I was with him for one of these latter speeches and could see that they tired him deeply. Not to mention the hassles of post-9/11 travel and the crush of fame.

Toward the end he'd apologize for not giving autographs. *Apologize,* in an age when celebrity athletes grandly sold them! And even here he'd make it a joke, saying that he'd always felt awkward at such occasions. For an author, writing out something was giving away a sample of his work, almost like a doctor passing out corpses. His listeners would laugh—and understand. That's how he found the strength to carry on speaking: for the pleasure of making people laugh, and the gratification of helping them understand.

Who else of his literary stature was doing this, after all? Somebody had better speak up, Kurt insisted. Plus there was his lingering fear that in old age he'd be forgotten, or written off as a relic of the 1960s. Events of the 1970s, '80s, and '90s were demonstrating the need for corrective comment. And even though his books remained relevant and could speak for themselves to several generations of readers, he still felt the need to get out there and make his points personally, to show his readers that he really cared.

He was always pleased that people listened. Especially young people. When critics challenged him about being able to change the minds of presidents, generals, and heads of corporations, Kurt would always reply that he was catching these people well before they achieved such rank and stature, reaching them while they were still young, when he could "poison their minds with humanity," a phrase he used from 1970 until his death. He felt he'd done this with some success before, but he was worried that the new millennium would find him puzzling, if not completely irrelevant. Time and again he'd lament the loss of a common stock of knowledge, regretting that his references to American history and culture would be missed. It pained him deeply when the time arrived when audiences would hear his quotation from Eugene V. Debs about sympathy for the unfortunates of this world and laugh, assuming it was a joke. And so he had to sharpen his points, make them more obvious, speaking with more fire and brimstone, as it were.

This new edge to his work brought him success. *A Man without a Country* (2005), published as an incidental small-press item, astonished everyone by becoming a best seller. Oldsters, checking out what the younger generation was watching on *The Daily Show* with Jon Stewart and *The Late Show* with David Letterman, were surprised to see an old favorite from their own younger days regaling hosts and audiences with amusing yet sharply biting comments on the day's state of affairs. It should have surprised no one that Kurt Vonnegut fit right into this new context, for his commitment since publishing his first story in 1950 had been to his times. Times change, of course, and so certain aspects of Vonnegut's delivery would change as well. But essences remain the same, and it was a reminder of this that Kurt was there to insist on. We're Americans, he'd say, and Americans are fundamentally decent people. So for God's sake let's start acting that way again.

I'd known Kurt personally since the early 1970s—from when the war in Vietnam was still being waged, for God's sake—and stayed close to him right up to the end. Others of his generation seemed to be mellowing. One of my research interests, the memoirs of World War II pilots, had put me in contact with a large group of people Kurt's age, and so I could measure the reaction of his generation to successive events of my own and of my children. Most took it all in stride. But not Kurt Vonnegut. Nixon's shenanigans he took as dark humor, Reagan's indulgences as annoying. But when President George Bush, the first President Bush, initiated the first Gulf War, Kurt nearly went off his rocker.

"I've never seen him so angry," our mutual friend Dan Wakefield reported after a New York visit. Bob Weide, working on his Vonnegut documentary, told me the same. But at least that war ended quickly, and the grand old man settled down.

A decade later, things got much worse. But Kurt's anger was either slower to rise, or was measured at the start in proportion to the heights it would scale before the end.

Early evidence was in his response to the 9/11 events. Not surprisingly, he viewed them as a human tragedy. His first published comments were in his neighborhood's local newsletter, in an account of a memorial service for the firefighters from the area's ladder company who'd rushed downtown to the Trade Center buildings and had perished in the first's collapse. In New York terms, that loss had happened far away, so Kurt turned it around to make it closely personal. The year before, he recalled, this same ladder company had answered a call in their own neighborhood, to put out an unwelcome fire on the top floor of Kurt's townhouse, where he'd left a cigarette butt smoldering in a wastepaper basket. To make things worse, he'd gone back into the room trying to extinguish the blaze himself, and he was overcome by the smoke. The firefighters had not only saved his house, but saved his life.

Some of those brave people were among those who'd died at ground zero, he noted. But he didn't stop there. Firefighters around the world were surely putting out unwelcome fires at this moment, some of them in Afghanistan. And so he was remembering them, too.

The news media went nuts with this. Who, in the solemn aftermath of 9/11, when "United We Stand" was a universal mantra, could be pitying the Taliban? Or so it seemed. For his statement, Kurt Vonnegut was widely reviled. Times were indeed changing.

Not that Vonnegut changed. The war in Iraq displeased him even more, but what upset him the most was how just thinking about it in rational terms was now deeply frowned upon, if not forbidden.

Case in point: being interviewed in New York by a reporter from Australia's national newspaper shortly after the Bali bombing (in which many Australians perished), Kurt was asked to agree that suicide bombers had to be insane, or at least to have no feelings at all—to be brainless automatons, or some such. There could certainly be no human satisfaction in the act, no sense to it at all.

Kurt disagreed. There had to be an incredible thrill to the act, he speculated. Even a sense of purpose, given the political and religious motivation. He could easily see how someone so committed to a believed-in cause could do this.

The Australian news media went berserk, taking an incidental comment from the much longer interview and making it headline material, a classic out-of-context smear. I wasn't surprised Kurt had said this. Much earlier he'd explained the thrill of preparing for combat, of being a member of a group fully armed and heading to the front. This from a confirmed pacifist! To the Australian reporter, he'd simply tried to answer a question in reasonable fashion. Common sense dictated that there had to be some explanation for young Americans aspiring to combat in the front lines (where it was inevitable many of them would perish, as did happen in the case Vonnegut describes, the Battle of the Bulge). Just as reason suggested that suicide bombers had to have some sense of purpose for what they did. But for the present, common sense was ruled out. Don't dare identify with the enemy as human beings. They aren't, or at least are not sane ones. They have to be crazy to be opposing us. End of story.

People were not thinking, the author believed, when they were allowing a government under President George W. Bush to wage such an unconscionable if not outrightly ridiculous war. This explains much of the anger in *A Man without a Country*. How can an entire country believe that Middle Easterners hate us because of our free democracy and would destroy us for that, and not the more reasonable possibility that they're simply angry for us interfering with their own part of the world? It seems so elemental, no more complex than mourning the death of a selfless firefighter *anywhere,* or of believing that young Muslims can be no less willing to sacrifice their lives than young Americans. But, in these times, such clear thought seemed strictly out-of-bounds.

Many of the short essays collected in *A Man without a Country* first appeared in the biweekly journal *In These Times,* an appropriate title for Kurt's attempts at reason. In 2005, when the volume became such a great success, he acted modestly, claiming that he'd only written the pieces at the urging of the journal's editor, Joel Bleifuss (who insisted Vonnegut's thoughts were needed, that his voice had to be heard), and that they were only now being collected because Dan Simon of Seven Stories Press made the project happen.

In fact Kurt was—as always—eager to speak out and convinced that what he had to say was important. Earlier in the decade, as these pieces appeared, he'd sent me photocopies, sometimes of his faxed typescript to the journal, other times of the published copy. Peter Reed, Bob Weide, and others presumably got these as well. *He wanted us to know what he was doing.* Then, on April 15, 2003, a bigger package arrived, comprising photocopies of nine *In These Times* essays (most of which he'd already sent separately) and his typescript of a widely advertised Clemens Lecture forthcoming at the Mark Twain House in Hartford, Connecticut. I'm sure others got it too, but mine was inscribed "Dear Jerry Klinkowitz—Here is what I did in the war just won. I thank you for your many years of encouragement. Cheers! Kurt Vonnegut."

The "war just won" was the Iraq War, the declaration of victory just one of the president's repeated statements of success, which had started with the infamous "mission accomplished" boast. The material Kurt sent included comments on the war but ranged much wider. Yet all of it pertained to the country's condition at the moment. And, most important, Kurt was collecting those comments for friends of his to read, not as separate pieces but as an organized statement. He wanted to be heard. And so he was, albeit in quasi-*samizdat* form. Perhaps he was implying that conditions in the United States had deteriorated to those of the Soviet Union in cold-war days, that, given media reaction to his simple calls for plain common sense, he'd resorted to private circulation of copied papers.

Therefore I wasn't surprised when *A Man without a Country* appeared two-and-one-half years later. Maybe Dan Simon at Seven Stories Press had been on Kurt's mailing list too, and perhaps it was true that Simon initiated and shepherded the project. But there was no doubt but that Kurt wanted the material collected and presented to the public as a book. This time he didn't have to be cajoled, but came up with the idea himself. This time he really wanted it as part of his canon.

And so it was, as the concluding piece.

As discussed in my introduction to *Kurt Vonnegut's America*, his anger in *A Man without a Country* is ultimately mollified a bit by the humor he finds in situations, even if the last resort is reducing the president and his top men to the status of vulgar toilet-function humor. Anything for a laugh—and reasonably so, as laughter was all that was left to put things in perspective. Reason sure hadn't worked. By 2005 perhaps the 9/11 solemnity could be jiggled a bit by urging people to put flags everywhere as a defensive measure, that doing so would be sure to scare the terrorists away. At least no reviewers—and the book was widely reviewed—complained this time around. Probably because by the end of 2005 America was ready for some common sense to be talked to it.

Kurt never let anger reduce himself to an issue-driven propaganda machine. He never let it make him anything less than the full human being he was. And that fullness included, in his case, almost impeccably good manners. These manners were practiced for the best of reasons: simple common decency. For all his railings about the Bushes, father and son, he was nevertheless charmed, even moved, when after giving a graduation address at Rice University in Houston, Texas, a member of the audience wrote him a fan letter. It had been the best such address she'd ever heard, the letter writer assured him. And this was a sentiment shared by her husband and several other family members in attendance.

Who wrote the letter? Barbara Bush.

Kurt sent me a copy. As a joke? No. He was proud of it and had written her back with thanks. A copy of that letter was enclosed too. *Samizdat.* But of a type that tells us there's hope.

How on earth could Kurt Vonnegut, especially the Kurt Vonnegut who was stewing away in anger at the Bushes in *A Man without a Country,* not only maintain such courtesy with the former First Lady but be proud of it as well? I knew the answer, and it was back in the volume John Somer and I had cajoled him into publishing in 1974, *Wampeters, Foma & Granfalloons.* It's from his essay "Good Missiles, Good Manners, Good Night," that had first appeared in the *New York Times* editorial page for September 13, 1969. That had been at the peak of protest against the Vietnam War, when a large part of the country was as angry with the government as Kurt was now in 2005. In 1969, writing for the *Times,* Kurt noted that he'd just discovered that an old high school classmate of his was presently married to Melvin Laird, the secretary of defense and front man for the government's war policy.

What did he do—phone her for a bawling out? Not at all. He'd actually sent a note to his old friend suggesting that they meet when he was visiting Washington, D.C.

"There was no reply," Kurt tells his readers. "Maybe Mrs. Laird's supposed enthusiasm for my work was a hoax." But he adds this, which is what we should keep in mind when considering his courtesy to that other fan, Barbara Bush:

> Word of honor—if I had been invited into the Laird home, I would have smiled and smiled. I would have understood that the defense establishment was only doing what it had to do, no matter how suicidally. I would have agreed, hearing the other fellow's side of the story, that even for planets there are worse things than death. Upon leaving, I would have thanked the Lairds for a nice time. I would have said, "I only regret that my wife couldn't have been here, too. She would have loved it."
>
> I would have thanked God, too, that no members of the younger generation were along. Kids don't learn nice manners in high school anymore. If they met a person who was in favor of building a device which would cripple and finally kill all children everywhere, they wouldn't smile. They would bristle with hatred, which is rude. (105)

The context for these comments is a friend's observation that not only were the people presently (in 1969) running things the folks that he and Kurt went to high school with, but by their age they have caught on that life is nothing but high school. It's a good way of familiarizing the unfamiliar, getting things back into a perspective from which they can be measured. As for those high-schoolers and college kids of 1969 that Vonnegut worried about offending, they're the ones now running the country—and thank God he got to some of them back then, poisoning their minds with humanity so there could at least be some opposition to the others he hadn't reached. But a third of a century later, he was reaching their mother. And apparently she'd had some of her grandchildren along for that speech at Rice. Hope blooms eternal. Good manners still open doors. And, once opened, good sense can start doing the rest.

Opening doors had not always been easy, or even possible, as is apparent from some early work now come to light. In the year following his father's death, Mark Vonnegut ("my son the doctor," as Kurt had become fond of calling him) sorted through old files his mother had kept at the family's home in West Barnstable, gathering enough coherent material to satisfy Putnam's as the second volume owed them on a two-book contract for which Vonnegut had been paid. His projected novel, *If God Were Alive Today*, proved to be unwriteable. Peter Reed's editing of *Bagombo Snuff Box* in 1999 satisfied the first obligation, and now *Armageddon in Retrospect* (2008) would save Kurt's estate from having to pay back a considerable advance for the second. Mark's introduction is affectionate, and he does a son's duty well by delivering in person (and reprinting as well) the speech his father was scheduled to give in Indianapolis the month he died. As a way of contextualizing the collection's stories and essays about World War II, Mark also reprinted one of the letters Kurt sent me to use in my own study, *Slaughterhouse-Five: Reforming the Novel and the World* (1990). It dates from 1945. The other pieces, written in the late 1940s and early 1950s, are interesting but emphatically noncanonical, having been rejected many times over: by the magazines that had been taking Kurt's early work, by his agents (Kenneth Littauer and Max Wilkinson) who didn't wish to reach any farther down in the market, and by Kurt himself six times when assembling the stories for *Canary in a Cat House*, *Welcome to the Monkey House*, and *Bagombo Snuff Box* or the essays for *Wampeters, Foma & Granfalloons*, *Palm Sunday*, and *Fates Worse Than Death*.

As a scholarly resource, which is how *Armageddon in Retrospect* is best viewed, the book shows us two things: first of all, that the American public of the early 1950s was not yet ready for a pacifistic response to World War II, and, second, that Kurt Vonnegut's unique method for dealing with the war had not yet been developed. The former clarifies how these stories were not marketable, while the latter tells why the author never put them in his collections, several of which would include other unpublished or market-rejected works.

The weaknesses are readily apparent. Some of the stories are unjustifiably sentimental—not tempered with irony as are "D.P." and "Long Walk to Forever," which passed muster for *Welcome to the Monkey House,* but instead exploiting things like the bathos of a crippled child's pet rabbit being killed and eaten by soldiers (American soldiers, no less, as happens in "Spoils"). This story and others rely on demeaning stereotypes, including air-head wives; it's a shallow woman who prompts her husband's discomforting memories in "Spoils," and an even shallower one who aggravates her mate in "The Unicorn Trap." Most are awkwardly obvious, from the predictable fascination a little boy has for military hardware in "Happy Birthday, 1951" to the behavior patterns of soldiers, which in several stories revolve about pillaging and looting. When these same soldiers are shown as prisoners of war, their themes are reductive, with food more lusted for than women, and privileges obtained by collaboration with the guards. *Stalag 17,* anyone? At worst, opinions are stated in essaylike fashion, as in "The Commandant's Desk," where a humiliated cabinetmaker in soft focus speaks lines fashioned for Will Geer.

The matter of Dresden is reserved for an essay, "Wailing Shall Be in All Streets," but it is unlike any essay Kurt would include in *Wampeters, Foma & Granfalloons* or later collections. Paragraphs are long, consisting of long sentences. There are no quirky jumps or sudden juxtapositions—no surprises, in other words, just a stolid recounting of the facts, as if the facts alone should be enough. By the time he wrote *Slaughterhouse-Five,* the author had learned to his great sorrow that facts alone were never enough. Facts could be conveniently ignored. Surprises couldn't be.

Kurt's family was surely surprised when they received his letter from repatriation camp. Dated May 29, 1945, it's drafted in an entirely different language than this collection's Dresden essay or any of its stories. There's nothing the least sentimental about it, just the news of what's happened to him since being captured by Wehrmacht soldiers the previous December. But neither does he expect that the facts will speak for themselves. He arranges them artfully, ending each description of casualties incurred along the way with a tagline that speaks volumes: "But not me." Anticipating the mantra from *Slaughterhouse-Five,* "So it goes," it lets the author make a comment minimally, even mutely, like the pregnant silences in Jack Benny's radio routines or the facial expressions of Laurel and Hardy. He's showing how there's a grim comedy to his survival, a preposterous irony in the fact that he should be writing from a base called Camp Lucky Strike while having his body weight restored with milk shakes. It has been a children's crusade. But at least he's coming home.

What's the biggest difference between Kurt's letter to his family in 1945 and the subsequent pieces he wrote but failed to get published? The latter he modeled on industry standards of the day, sentimentality and obviousness and stereotypes included, without risking any of the innovations that would challenge, however subversively, the way business at *Collier's* and the *Saturday Evening Post* was being done. His single departure from these modes was the pacifism theme, which was not only more than a decade ahead of its time but awkward to express within a conventional format. In the letter, however, he sounds like a person from Indianapolis. With his family in mind as readers, he uses this voice naturally. Not until later would he find ways of using it for the American people at large.

Near the end of the coda in *Bagombo Snuff Box*, Kurt listed some of his fellow midwesterners whose vernacular culture he admired, One of them was, like his father and grandfather, an architect, no less a person than Frank Lloyd Wright. This man was a writer as well as an architect, sustaining himself and his family by publication when, during years of personal crisis and then during the Great Depression, there were no commissions for building, yet also during his years of architectural triumph, early and late, when he wished to advocate his method and the philosophy behind it. In analyzing that writing, critic Baker Brownell, in his book *The Human Community* (1950), offers a commentary that applies perfectly to Kurt Vonnegut's work as well:

> His prose may not be subtle, but it has power. It may lack craft, but it flows from one source. It may not have linear continuity, but it has spiritual coherence and a proud though harsh integrity. His prose is not sensitive to the materials that the [conventional] writer must use. . . . But his language is direct. And if he is blank sometimes to verbal distinction, quality, and sound, he is also blank to the worn dance routines, the timed kicks and fillips of the professional word masters of our day.
>
> On the background of the thousands of fully written books and articles, raised like a screen to filter the sun, produced with endless competence in all the professionally tested modes, Wright's prose is somehow naked and revelatory. It is direct, whole, abruptly real. Though it is not always professional or fluid, nor even competent, his prose has the sting and substance, not of a book, but of a man.
>
> It is integral rather than linear. It lacks the marching rhythms and proximate coherence of style that goes, as it were, from one place to the next. His words shift and run like quicksilver under his hands. They bulge beyond his control, and their damned plasticity makes fixation of meaning for him, or definition, impossible. But his style has the kind of

spherical continuity, wholeness, the mystical or spiritual coherence, that often mark great work.

Wright, indeed, is never mainly linear in his thinking but integral. Because his thinking lacks connectives, it seems saltatory. Because it is not a line or linkage of one thing related to the next thing in terms only of those two things, his conversation seems to be a series of pounces. The things that he writes emerge abruptly like divers from under the water. They come up like bubbles. They have radial organization rather than surface continuity. Because his thought is integrated on other levels, the visible bubbles seem to have little continuity with one another. (236–37)

Brownell concludes that Wright writes this way because architecture itself as a field values the rhythms of space and matter above time and the movements of words. Kurt Vonnegut always introduced himself as the son and grandson of architects, trained by his father to see in buildings what others might miss. This disposition may be what Brownell describes as the ability to perceive relationships "in terms not of one line of functions or causes but of many." The structure of both Wright's and Vonnegut's written work, then, is of a body, not a line: "Each item of it refers not merely to its proximate predecessor and successor but in a multitude of imitations to all the members of the group" (237).

My last exchange with Kurt Vonnegut involved Frank Lloyd Wright as a subject and took place in late November and early December of 2006, three months before the fall that robbed him of consciousness and four before his death. He was as up and as eager as ever, with none of the fatigue and depression that had colored his moods a few years earlier. I think the success of *A Man without a Country* heartened him, but just being cheered up reenergized him for the work that still needed to be done.

I'd written him about a fugitive essay on the painter Jimmy Ernst that collector André Eckenrode had tipped me off to, and asked, almost as a postscript, if he'd ever had much interest in the work of Frank Lloyd Wright (I'd forgotten about the reference in *Bagombo Snuff Box*). As always, Kurt replied the same day he got my letter; fellow Luddites, neither of us used computers, much less e-mail. He identified the Ernst piece in a short paragraph, informative and precise, yet garnished with something not in the essay but "what I often said about him in ordinary conversations: That he was the only member of the Academy [of Arts and Letters] whose father had excelled in the very same art."

There was the segue to Wright, just in the manner that Baker Brownell describes. Ernst's father the painter, like father like son. Wright the architect, like Kurt's father—two of Wright's sons were architects, a profession young Kurt was not allowed to pursue, despite his desire to do so and become his father's partner. Kurt thus finished the page with three more paragraphs plus his standard farewell. But it turns out Kurt really wanted to chat about the man. Two weeks later, after the hubbub of his eighty-fourth birthday, on the eve of which he'd written me, he phoned me at home. It must have been late in the evening, because we'd set the answering machine and gone to bed.

Well, he'd been famous all his life for late-night phone calls, so I wasn't surprised to be retrieving this one the next morning. He'd wanted to add some thoughts to those expressed in his letter: that Frank Lloyd Wright was impudent, always putting on a show. How on earth was he allowed to do that? Kurt didn't know how, but he sure was fun. Could I call him back tomorrow?

I did. At 9:40 A.M. his time he picked up the phone on the first ring, saying "Good morning." Talk about service with a smile! He had a lot to add about Wright. That he was an entertainer, something that rated high in Kurt's book: "That's why we're here on earth, to entertain." As stock-market people say in their own language, Wright was a "contrarian," a maker of practical jokes who loved fun, just like jazz, and reveled in getting away with it. His architecture danced like action painting. Kurt's own father despised him, got enraged about him. Not as a daily issue, but when young Kurt would "pull father's chain" by asking, when something like Fallingwater would be in the news, "why can't you do something like that?"

Kurt admitted that he knew Wright best from the Guggenheim Museum, a structure of extreme self-indulgence. But he also knew the Usonian houses were practical and affordable. "He did something for the common man, like Charles Eames and his Eames chair, a great comfort to sit in after a day's work." Or in which to do a day's work: because publisher Seymour Lawrence was asking Kurt to read and evaluate so many manuscripts, he'd given into requests and bought his author an Eames chair, the first of three he'd own.

Finally, some words about his upcoming speech in Indianapolis, where he was to be honored this next April with the commencement of a year-long festival. His theme, he said, would be "what constitutes 'progress.'" Sometimes "progress" looks ironic, as in the execution of criminals, where lethal injection serves as a step forward from hanging or gassing. Other times it seems silly, as when in art, after centuries of European mastery, "we finally get our own," and who steps to the fore but Jackson Pollock, "spreading a canvas on his garage floor and dribbling on it."

Would he include Frank Lloyd Wright in his Indianapolis talk, as interested as he seemed to be in him now? Kurt "really didn't know his practical housing," and so didn't feel qualified. But what he'd said in his letter a few weeks before was enough for me:

As for Frank Lloyd Wright: My own father, an architect about twenty years Wright's junior, found him a showman and a publicity hound, whose structures celebrated himself rather than the needs of anyone who might inhabit one. "Falling Waters" [*sic*], for example, is in fact inhospitable because of the water. Of his "Prairie Houses," one of which I saw near the University of Chicago, the late critic Brendan Gill said that if there had been no basements or attics, Wright would have invented them. The one I saw was a trophy for its owner, like a Picasso, say, but otherwise not at all that comforting.

And Wright's only structure in this city, "The Guggenheim," with its dominant lines aslant, is the worse possible space for paintings. Wright, I am told, asked his Prairie House clients not to spoil his interiors with framed art. I am told, too, that on a tour of a display of abstract expressionist paintings in another museum here, maybe the Whitney, he actually struck one work with his cane, knocking off a chunk of impasto.

I loved him. He was fun for me and a lot of other people, was "jazz," if you like, but surely not for my father. As for real jazz, which saved my life, my father called it "jungle music."

In any case, cheers, Jerry.

BIBLIOGRAPHY

Books by Kurt Vonnegut

Player Piano. New York: Scribner's, 1952.

The Sirens of Titan. New York: Dell, 1959.

Canary in a Cat House. Greenwich, Conn.: Fawcett, 1961.

Mother Night. Greenwich, Conn.: Fawcett, 1961. The preferred text for quotations is the hardcover edition that followed the paperback original; it was published in New York by Harper & Row in 1966, with a new introduction by the author.

Cat's Cradle. New York: Holt, Rinehart & Winston, 1963.

God Bless You, Mr. Rosewater. New York: Holt, Rinehart & Winston, 1965.

Welcome to the Monkey House. New York: Delacorte Press / Seymour Lawrence, 1968.

Slaughterhouse-Five. New York: Delacorte Press / Seymour Lawrence, 1969.

Happy Birthday, Wanda June. New York: Delacorte Press / Seymour Lawrence, 1971.

Between Time and Timbuktu. New York: Delacorte Press / Seymour Lawrence, 1972.

Breakfast of Champions. New York: Delacorte Press / Seymour Lawrence, 1973.

Wampeters, Foma & Granfalloons. New York: Delacorte Press / Seymour Lawrence, 1974.

Slapstick. New York: Delacorte Press / Seymour Lawrence, 1976.

Jailbird. New York: Delacorte Press / Seymour Lawrence, 1979.

Palm Sunday. New York: Delacorte Press / Seymour Lawrence, 1981.

Deadeye-Dick. New York: Delacorte Press / Seymour Lawrence, 1982.

Galápagos. New York: Delacorte Press / Seymour Lawrence, 1985.

Bluebeard. New York: Delacorte Press, 1987.

Hocus Pocus. New York: Putnam's, 1990.

Fates Worse Than Death. New York: Putnam's, 1991.

Timequake. New York: Putnam's, 1997.

Bagombo Snuff Box. New York: Putnam's, 1999.

God Bless You, Dr. Kevorkian. New York: Seven Stories Press, 1999.

A Man without a Country. New York: Seven Stories Press, 2005.

Armageddon in Retrospect. New York: Putnam's, 2008.

Bibliography

Secondary Sources

Brownell, Baker. *The Human Community.* New York: Harper, 1950.

Hicks, Granville. "Literary Horizons: *Slaughterhouse-Five.*" *Saturday Review* 52, xiii (29 March 1969): 25.

Klinkowitz, Jerome. *Slaughterhouse-Five: Reforming the Novel and the World.* Boston: G. K. Hall / Twayne, 1990.

Klinkowitz, Jerome, and John Somer, eds. *Innovative Fiction.* New York: Dell, 1972.

————, eds. *The Vonnegut Statement.* New York: Delacorte Press / Seymour Lawrence, 1973.

Klinkowitz, Jerome, and Donald L. Lawler, eds. *Vonnegut in America.* New York: Delacorte Press / Seymour Lawrence, 1977.

Reed, Peter J. *The Short Fiction of Kurt Vonnegut.* Westport, Conn.: Greenwood Press, 1996.

Vonnegut, Mark. *The Eden Express: A Personal Account of Schizophrenia.* New York: Praeger, 1975.

Yarmolinsky, Jane Vonnegut. *Angels without Wings: A Courageous Family's Triumph over Tragedy.* Boston: Houghton Mifflin, 1987.

INDEX